"No longer little children, not quite independent adults, teenhood is the fast transition between the two. In all the changes, wise teens need straight talk—bold talk!—the kind of advice that is sharp enough to help them cut through the false promises and lies of our culture and blunt enough to push back all the old, tired stereotypes of teenagers. You found it! This book is fearless, lucid, God focused, and gospel drenched, all applied in concrete practices, and aimed at nothing less than your eternal joy. These precious years are not the time to slack off, Jaquelle says, they're the time to stand out. This book stands out as a valiant work from one teen serving other teens (and those who love them)!"

Tony Reinke, staff writer and researcher, desiringGod.org; author, *Lit! A Christian Guide to Reading Books* and *12 Ways Your Phone Is Changing You*

"In a culture where many young people feel entitled and struggle through swamps of victimization, Jaquelle Ferris calls her fellow teens to Christian discipline. She wants them to choose the hard tasks, the road of discipline, the life of obedience and service to Christ, in response to the gospel of grace. May she and her fellow visionaries—and there is a growing number of them!—follow this path to the end, empowered by transforming grace."

D. A. Carson, Research Professor of New Testament, Trinity Evangelical Divinity School; Cofounder, The Gospel Coalition

"Jaquelle Ferris writes her first book with this purpose: 'that the gospel will change your life, that you will surrender all to the cause of Christ.' That is a compelling purpose, and one that many teenagers will embrace wholeheartedly, thanks to this book. May Christ bless Jaquelle and use her book toward that glorious end!"

Ray Ortlund, Lead Pastor, Immanuel Church, Nashville, Tennessee; council member, The Gospel Coalition; President, Renewal Ministries; author, *Marriage and the Mystery of the Gospel*

"Jaquelle's zeal for the gospel is contagious. This book is enjoyable and practical, but the effect thereof is individual transformation with global ramifications. I pray that a multitude of teenagers would take up and read this book."

Gloria Furman, author, *The Pastor's Wife*, *Missional Motherhood*, and *Alive in Him*

"One of my hopes for the church is that we would take seriously those in the teen years, that we would speak to them as those capable of and accountable for understanding the implications of a vibrant faith. Jaquelle Ferris does this, and even better, she does so as a peer. In *This Changes Everything*, both Jaquelle's practical words and her positive example offer needed encouragement to other teens. And they deeply encouraged this mother of teens, as well."

Jen Wilkin, author, *Women of the Word* and *None Like Him*; Bible teacher

"Paul told Timothy to set an example and not let anyone despise his youth. Jaquelle is a young woman who embodies this truth and demonstrates the power of the gospel for young leaders. She describes her book as a chicken nugget. It's for those old enough to stop gumming baby food. She's right. There's a lot here to chew on. I recommend this book for both you and the young people in your life."

Dan DeWitt, Director, Center for Biblical Apologetics and Public Christianity, Cedarville University; author, *Christ or Chaos* and *Jesus or Nothing*

"In this gospel-saturated little book, Jaquelle gives a courageous and winsome call to young people to treasure Jesus above all, and to see how faith in him touches and transforms every area of life. Teens, I commend this book to you, as well as the witness of a godly young woman who is living boldly and openly for the glory of Jesus Christ and his life-changing gospel."

Jon Nielson, Ministry Director, Christian Union, Princeton University; co-editor, *Gospel-Centered Youth Ministry*

"Jaquelle Ferris is an outstanding writer, not just 'for a teenager,' but for anyone. Writing takes work, as does following Jesus, and in *This Changes Everything*, the author has done her work well. Reading this book was a pleasure; it's biblical, challenging, and refreshing. Jaquelle's heart comes across clearly, her theology is strong, and what she says about church is desperately needed. I highly recommend this book."

Randy Alcorn, Founder and Director, Eternal Perspective Ministries; author, *Heaven, The Treasure Principle*, and *The Ishbane Conspiracy*

"Jaquelle writes as a teenager to teenagers. She writes with skill, with passion, and with a firm grounding in Scripture. I could list the many strengths of her book, but perhaps the most effective endorsement is this: I will gladly give *This Changes Everything* to my own teenagers with confidence that it will be a blessing to them."

Tim Challies, blogger, Challies.com

"This is a great book written by a bright young person, where Jaquelle clearly shows that young people can and should be challenged with the gospel of Jesus Christ. In a brief and very readable text, the author explains what the gospel is—what it demands and how it saves more than how it benefits us. The message of the cross is not a pragmatic message but rather a radically transforming and life-giving message. Read this book and you will find what I just said to be true. I recommend it, especially for young people, parents, and young leaders."

Miguel Núñez, Senior Pastor, International Baptist Church, Santo Domingo, Dominican Republic; President, Wisdom & Integrity Ministries

"In a culture where teens have been given a free pass to live self-focused, immature, irresponsible lives, they desperately need to know that they were created for a bigger purpose. In *This Changes Everything*, Jaquelle brings the gospel to life by showing how relevant and applicable it is to our modern generation. This book is a must for all teens!"

Kristen Clark and Bethany Baird, Founders, Girl Defined Ministries; authors, *Girl Defined: God's Radical Design for Beauty, Femininity, and Identity*

"Powerful! Packed with the fundamental values of the Christian faith, *This Changes Everything* does an excellent job presenting what truly matters most to my generation. A simple yet profound book, I would recommend *This Changes Everything* to any young person eager to start taking their faith seriously."

Trent Blake, age 17, Mulberry, Florida

"We teenagers are at a confusing and impressionable place in our culture. Without clear direction on why and how we should be living as Christians, it's easy to just give up. With plenty of real-life illustrations, *This Changes Everything* clearly explains why the gospel matters so much and challenges us to live for the glory of God."

Olivia White, age 13, Mebane, North Carolina

"So often, as teenagers, we get caught up in school, sports, and other activities and forget that our lives should really be about God. In this book, Jaquelle points us back to the Creator of all things and his wonderful plan for us. And she doesn't just leave it as ushy-gushy feelings. With a humble attitude, she shows what it looks like to take this good news and allow it to transform our lives. I highly recommend this book!"

Jason Zimmerman, age 16, Ithaca, New York

"This book was phenomenal. Jaquelle writes personally and she has a way of making you think deeper than is comfortable. As a young Christian myself, this book cut straight through me and gave me a deeper yearning for Christ, as well as practical ways to live a life more like Christ's. She is on point with everything she says and uses the Bible as the basis for everything."

Emma Roth, age 17, Grafton, Ohio

This Changes Everything

THIS CHANGES EVERYTHING

How the Gospel Transforms the Teen Years

JAQUELLE FERRIS

CROSSWAY®

WHEATON, ILLINOIS

This Changes Everything: How the Gospel Transforms the Teen Years

Published by Crossway
1300 Crescent Street
Wheaton, Illinois 60187

Cover design: Micah Lanier

First printing 2017

Reprinted with new cover 2025

Printed in the United States of America

All emphases in Scripture quotations have been added by the author.

Hardcover ISBN: 978-1-4335-5514-5
ePub ISBN: 978-1-4335-5517-6
PDF ISBN: 978-1-4335-5515-2
Mobipocket ISBN: 978-1-4335-5516-9
Trade paperback ISBN: 979-8-8749-0654-2

Library of Congress Cataloging-in-Publication Data

Names: Ferris, Jaquelle, 1997- author.
Title: This changes everything : how the gospel transforms the teen years / Jaquelle Ferris.
Description: Wheaton, Illinois : Crossway, [2017] | Includes bibliographical references.
Identifiers: LCCN 2016041878 (print) | LCCN 2017005229 (ebook) | ISBN 9781433555145 (PDF) | ISBN 9781433555176 (ePub) | ISBN 9781433555169 (Mobipocket) | ISBN 9781433555152 (pdf) | ISBN 9781433555169 (mobi) | ISBN 9781433555176 (epub)
Subjects: LCSH: Teenagers—Religious life. | Christian life.
Classification: LCC BV4531.3 .C765 2017 (print) | LCC BV4531.3 (ebook) | DDC 248.8/3—dc23
LC record available at https://lccn.loc.gov/2016041878

Crossway is a publishing ministry of Good News Publishers.

BP 35 34 33 32 31 30 29 28 27 26 25
13 12 11 10 9 8 7 6 5 4 3 2 1

To my parents,
Sean and Diana Crowe.
Thank you for teaching me the gospel.
This is your book too.

CONTENTS

INTRODUCTION

I like football movies. I also like to read books. I run a lot. I love sushi and dark chocolate and hate coffee (don't judge me). I have a younger brother, and most days we get along pretty well. When I'm bored I scroll through Twitter on my phone, or sometimes Instagram. I have two cats who are my babies. I don't like cleaning the bathroom. I'm terrible at dancing—yet I still constantly do it. My name is Jaquelle, and I'm a teenager.

But that's not the most important thing about me. The biggest, most crucial, most significant thing I want you to know is that my life's task is to follow Jesus. To obey Jesus. To look for joy and satisfaction and peace in Jesus. Jesus is the One who changed my life.

That's what this book is about.

This Book Is a Chicken Nugget

Like all teenagers, I used to be a child. And before I was a child, I was a baby. Babies, as I'm sure you know, are not in the habit of eating chicken nuggets. They drink milk, and they gum mush. That's what I was once. Then my teeth grew in, and slowly but surely I was able to eat and digest solid food. It was an exciting day when I matured from strained peas to chicken nuggets. It marked a milestone in my growth.

This Changes Everything is, in my mind, a chicken nugget.

It's for young people who are Christians but no longer gumming spiritual baby food. We've eaten the basics and are still hungry for more. We're ready for meat and reject the fluff so often pressed on us. We really don't want to be talked down to. We want to know how to live a godly life as teenagers and as Christians, and we don't want to be spoon-fed when we're ready to dig in ourselves.

Many people in our society (and even our church culture) would say that we're not ready. Teenagers are too young, we're too inexperienced, we could never understand theology, or we'd be too bored. These are supposed to be our fun years, they say, our easy years. Why would we tackle the tough chicken nuggets of truth when milk is perfectly acceptable?

My answer: because we love Jesus. If we love Jesus, we'll love truth, and we'll want to grow. We'll reject the status quo. These aren't our rebellious years; these are the years we rise up to obey the call of Christ. This isn't our time to slack off; it's our time to stand out. This isn't a season for self-satisfaction; it's a season for God-glorification. Our youth is by God's grace, in God's hands, and for God's fame. He is the whole point of our lives.

So are you ready to dig in?

What's This Book About?

There are eight chapters in this book, each structured around a common theme in a Christian's life and each grounded in how the gospel effects change. First, we look at our identity as Jesus-followers and why *who* we are influences *what* we do. Then we study our story, the gospel—which is really God's story, life changing and magnificent—in chapter 2. Chapter 3 is our community, the church, and where our place is in it. Chapter 4 is about our common sins, especially the "respectable" kind, and what our attitude toward them should be.

The fifth chapter is our disciplines, the difficult tasks we do out of love for God and a desire for godliness. Chapter 6 is how we grow in Christ, and chapter 7 is how we spend our time. Chapter 8 is our relationships with others—our parents, our siblings, our friends, and members of the opposite gender.

My Hope for You

Writers often hear this piece of advice: write the book you want to read. I'll tell you right now: this is the book I've wanted to read for a long time. From one teenager to another, from one Jesus-follower to another, this is what I've learned from God's Word about living a joy-fueled, obedience-filled, and Christ-exalting life while I'm young. My hope is that you'll find a friend and a helper in me. My prayer is that the gospel will change your life, that you will surrender all to the cause of Christ. My desire is that together you and I will follow Jesus every day—and nothing will ever be the same again.

1

OUR IDENTITY

Has anything ever changed your life?

I can think of a handful of moments that changed mine. My little brother's birth, for one. Starting my first job. Moving to Texas. Finding out my grandmother had cancer. Passing my driver's test. Getting accepted into college. Sending my first article into TheRebelution.com.

I know you've had your share of life-changing moments too. You started a new school or got your first car or met someone famous or went somewhere cool. You know what they are. From the impressive to the seemingly insignificant, we've all had these remarkable moments that shifted our perspectives and, in some way, changed our lives. They springboarded us in new directions or launched us on new paths.

But while these moments made important marks on our lives, they never changed us in our entirety. We were still the same people. We looked the same and talked the same and believed most of the same things.

That's what makes Jesus different.

Jesus changes everything about a person's life, from the obvious to the unseen. He shatters black and white into brilliant color and shakes the asleep until they're wide awake. Jesus-followers don't live like they did before following him. We don't talk about the same things or read the same books. We no longer dress or act or think the same way. Jesus makes people one hundred percent new. He takes the spiritually dead and makes us thrillingly, beautifully, and abundantly alive.

There's a Problem

But this is where we encounter a problem. There are people all across our world—from magazine cover celebrities to the soccer mom down the street to perhaps that person who occupies the locker next to yours—who claim to follow Jesus but actually don't. While saying they have hearts devoted to a passionate pursuit of God, they live unchanged lives. Indifferent lives. Lives that blend in, conform to, and meld with the world. Jesus changed nothing in their lives.

And this problem is getting bigger. Drew Dyck, a Christian author and editor, once heard this message at a youth conference: "Being a Christian isn't hard. . . . You won't lose your friends or be unpopular at school. Nothing will change. Your life will be the same, just better." Drew was stunned, but apparently the teenagers weren't. In fact, they weren't even listening, instead they were flicking Doritos at each other. Drew couldn't help but think, "And why should they? . . . Who cares about something that involves no adventure, no sacrifice, and no risk?"[1]

If Jesus changes nothing, they're right. Who cares about

Christianity? But the opposite is true too. If Jesus changes everything, following him is worth risking all. And that's the truth. If you take away one thing from this book, let it be this: *Jesus has no half-hearted followers.* He demands all. And when he saves you, he changes it all. The inevitable question is only—How?

How This Changed Paul's Life

Meet Paul. He was born like you and me—a sinner, with a tiny fist curled in rebellion against God that grew to be a giant fist that declared, "I hate Jesus so much, I'm going to persecute his followers." An incalculable antagonist to Jesus, Paul wanted to squelch his following. He wanted Christians dead, and he worked against them every step of the way. And then Jesus found him and said, "Paul, you are mine" (see Acts 9). Like the sudden snap of a switch, the Jesus-hater became a Jesus-follower.

Everything in Paul's life swiftly and radically changed. His life and dreams and ideologies and passions and motives and work were twisted inside out, irreversibly upended. Once persecuting Christians, he now became their greatest champion. He dropped his old life and followed Jesus to a brand-new but much happier life of global missions, church planting, and preaching about Jesus to anyone who would listen.

The Spirit of God also inspired him to author thirteen books of the New Testament. In one of these books, a letter to the church in the ancient city of Philippi, Paul gave a definition of what a Jesus-follower—a Christian—is. It's long, but he packed in everything. Read it carefully.

> Indeed, I count everything as loss because of the surpassing worth of knowing Christ Jesus my Lord. For his sake I have suffered the loss of all things and count them as rubbish, in order that I may gain Christ and be found in him, not having

> a righteousness of my own that comes from the law, but that which comes through faith in Christ, the righteousness from God that depends on faith—that I may know him and the power of his resurrection, and may share his sufferings, becoming like him in his death, that by any means possible I may attain the resurrection from the dead. (Phil. 3:8–11)

What is a Christian? According to Paul, a Christian is someone who does six things: (1) treasures Christ, (2) devalues everything else, (3) puts faith in Christ alone, (4) knows him, (5) suffers for him, and (6) becomes like him.

SIX THINGS A CHRISTIAN DOES (ACCORDING TO PAUL)

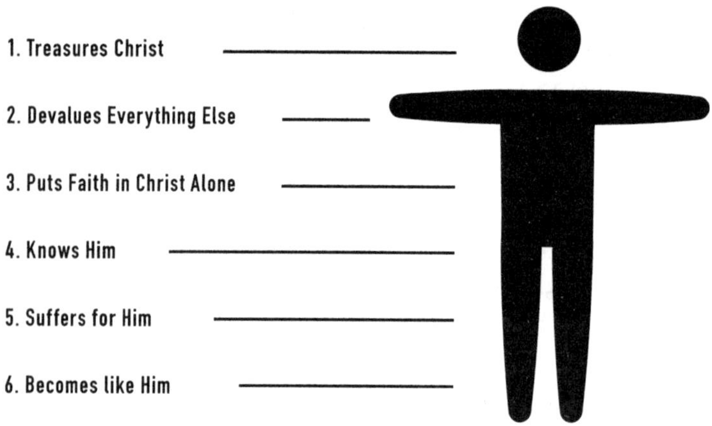

Christians Treasure Christ

Paul suggests that everything—even the most valuable, mind-blowingly awesome treasure out there—is worthless when compared with Jesus. Have you ever seen *National Treasure*? This movie follows a group of fictional American explorers who attempt to hunt down the greatest measurable treasure in the world—a collection of historical artifacts valued at billions of dollars. When they (*spoiler alert*) find it, the treasure is even more expensive and spectacular than they had imagined. Yet Paul says even this is nothing compared to Jesus.

Jim Elliot knew this well. A missionary to Ecuador in the 1950s, Jim was murdered by Huaorani Indians, the very people he was serving, before he turned twenty-nine years old. Here was a man who adored Jesus so much, he was willing to lose everything to tell others about him. Jim wrote a famous line that stands as a statement of his life: "He is no fool who gives what he cannot keep to gain that which he cannot lose."[2]

Jim knew he could only find soul-deep satisfaction when he recognized the ultimate worth of Jesus. He also knew that his Savior could never be casually regulated to a mere *part* of his life, compartmentalized like math class or football. Jesus *was* life. And that meant he was worth dying for.

But just as much, that meant he was worth living for. Most of us are probably not going to be martyred for our faith. Yet we can still take up our cross daily and follow Christ. No, we *must*. Christians are called to follow Jesus in death but equally in ordinary, uneventful, everyday life.

Christians Devalue Everything Else

When Paul says that he counts "everything as loss," maybe you think that he doesn't mean *everything*. What about the honor roll? Popularity? Comfort? Family? Friends? To Paul, that's like comparing fruit cores to a king's feast. They are indescribably inferior. No, that doesn't mean all of those things are necessarily sinful or unimportant; what it means is that when they are compared to Christ, they're nothing only because Jesus is everything.

Paul was the quintessential example of devaluing everything because of how much he treasured Christ. He suffered brutal shipwrecks and bloody beatings, lashings and imprisonments, starvation and snake bites, thirst, discomfort, loss, loneliness, and pain all because Jesus was worth it (2 Cor. 11:23–28). Jesus was better than safety. Jesus was better than health. Jesus was better than food. Jesus was better than friends. Paul counted everything as loss because Jesus was so much better than everything.

You and I, we have to look at our lives and ask ourselves, *Do I do that*? Do I live like Jesus is better than my phone? Is Jesus better than my body? Is Jesus better than makeup? Is Jesus better than sports? Would I gladly give it all up, without hesitation, for Jesus? Would I really?

While I'd love to quickly and confidently answer, "Yes, of course," I know my real response is too often, "Not really." Sure, there are beautiful moments when Jesus is supremely valuable to me, but then there are moments when he isn't. Those are the times I'm distracted from the treasure by trinkets and trifles. I'm too busy obsessing over how I look, or addictively checking my phone, or getting angry about a lost baseball game, and I'm living like Jesus is second best. Those are the times I most desperately need this reminder: Christ is my treasure. He's my reward, my joy, my everything. And as his follower, my task is to live like it.

Christians Have Faith in Him Alone

My brother Travis is a self-admitted rule follower. Down to the last letter of every law, state imposed or otherwise, he obeys. He won't even let me smuggle lollipops into the movie theater because the sign over there prohibits outside food and drink. It can be tempting for him, or others like him, to think that following rules will save him. If he can just be good enough or nice enough or, like Pinocchio, prove himself "selfless, brave, and true," he'll earn a shot at redemption. The lure is to trust in his own righteousness. But as a Jesus-follower and Jesus-treasurer, he's learned the ultimate futility of that misplaced trust. The Christian recognizes his own sinfulness and believes that only Christ's righteousness can rescue him from God's wrath (Gal. 2:16).

That's a counter-cultural message, though. We live in an age of self-help, where following your heart is the contemporary path to salvation. If you can just muster the strength and summon the courage, you've got this. You're the hero, the deliverer, and the savior. We're consistently told, *have faith in you* or *believe in yourself*.

Yet there may be no message more destructive to biblical Christianity. It is one so hideously and thoroughly rotted with self-idolatry that Jesus came to destroy it. Jesus came instead to call us to die daily to ourselves and trust in him as the true and perfect Savior (1 Pet. 2:24). So yes, have faith. Have great faith—but not in yourself. Have faith in Christ. Look to him. Ask his Spirit to give you unshakable and unwavering trust in him alone and then pursue it.

Christians Know Him

You cannot be a Christian unless you know God. Not just know *about* him. Even the demons know about God (James 2:19). You have to know him as Savior, as Lord, as Redeemer, as Justifier, as King, as Friend. A Christian has an intimate relationship with God. It's not one-sided, impersonal, surface level, or long distance. It's present and active and messy and real and fearful and divinely wonderful. It is a holy God loving imperfect humans and making a way for authentic communion with them.

This makes me think of Facebook. It took me until I was

nearly eighteen to get a Facebook account, and when I did I was pumped to connect with my friends. But then, slowly but surely, something else started happening. People who *weren't* my friends started sending me friend requests. We had mutual friends, or we were distant relatives, or we had met once at a barbecue, but we didn't know each other in "real life."

Being friends only on Facebook is weird, because even though I saw these peoples' pictures and their status updates and found myself learning quite a bit about their lives, I still didn't *know* them. I had never had a face-to-face conversation with them. I knew nothing beyond the flimsy superficial. I didn't know what their character was like, what their dreams were, or what they wanted most from life.

This is what it's like for those who claim to follow Jesus but don't actually know him. They can tell you he died on a cross. They say they pray to him sometimes. They listen to some Christian music and occasionally share Christian memes. But they don't know God relationally.

It's important to recognize that this is not God's fault. He gives us every opportunity to know him through his Word. That's where he reveals himself, his character boldly displayed on every page. Furthermore, he allows us to speak to him through prayer, a holy conduit of communication. Because Jesus removed God's wrath, he made a way for us to pray directly to God by his Spirit (Rom. 8:26–27).

A Christian knows these truths, loves these truths, and so communes with God personally and joyfully.

Christians Suffer for Him

To say that Christians won't suffer is a terrible lie. Suffering is a reality as certain as salvation itself. Just ask Paul or Jim Elliot

. . . or Jesus. When God saves you, you sacrifice a life of ease. "Then Jesus told his disciples, 'If anyone would come after me, let him deny himself and take up his cross and follow me'" (Matt. 16:24). Christians should expect suffering, while also recognizing that we have a great responsibility in the midst of it—to glorify God.

But it's hard for us to understand sometimes, isn't it? We hear the blood-stained stories of Christians in China and North Korea and the Middle East who are tortured and murdered for Jesus every day. We hear of their dramatic and horrific suffering, and we don't know what to make of it because that doesn't happen to those of us in the West. We get to go to church above ground. We get to pray in public places. We get to read our Bibles in front of police officers.

Yet that doesn't mean smaller bits of suffering for our faith won't happen. They will. We might be bullied because of our faith in Christ. We might be shamed. We might be fired from work or failed in a class. We might be mocked. We might be passed over for something good. We might lose friends. We might have to give up our dream school or dream job or dreams period. Suffering will come for the Jesus-follower. If it never does, that's a clue we're in trouble.

> Beloved, do not be surprised at the fiery trial when it comes upon you to test you, as though something strange were happening to you. But rejoice insofar as you share Christ's sufferings, that you may also rejoice and be glad when his glory is revealed. (1 Pet. 4:12–13)

Christians Become Like Him

Jesus-followers strive to become more holy as God's Spirit works in our hearts to make us more like him. We demonstrate our allegiance to Christ by daily conforming to his image (1 Pet. 1:15–16). And that's what the rest of this book is about: *the gospel changes everything.*

That means we understand the staggering weight of what God did for us, the depth of our sinfulness, and the height of God's mercy. That means we don't serve God in isolation. We join with the community of his church, and we become a family who lives to worship God together. That means that we run from sin—from our selfishness, gossip, insecurity, pride, lust, greed, discontentment, jealousy—and we repent and glory in grace. That means we cultivate disciplines in our lives that make us more like Jesus, reading and memorizing his Word, praying, and sharing the good news of the glorious gospel with others.

That means we grow in maturity through listening to biblically grounded sermons and soul-enriching music and reading books that inspire us to live kingdom-focused lives. That means we use our time in a way that is profitable, avoiding both laziness and sinful busyness and practicing self-denial. That means we foster relationships that will build us up by rejoicing in our family, nurturing good friendships, and considering romantic relationships from God's perspective.

That means that we love God more. Every day we die a little more to our old selves and live a little more like Christ (John 3:30). That's why we are called Christians, because we are of Christ, for Christ, with Christ, and in Christ alone.

Embracing Our Identity

Since we're young, now is the time we ask ourselves the ageless question: *Who am I?* Every person aches to know why they're here. We ask: *What is the thing that defines me? How am I supposed to live?* We look around and see all these people who call themselves Jesus-followers yet find their identity in material success or good grades or popularity or clothes or their bodies or their interests or their parents' expectations. The truth for us is that Jesus-followers, young and old and anywhere in between, can only find their identity in Jesus.

> From now on, therefore, we regard no one according to the flesh. Even though we once regarded Christ according to the flesh, we regard him thus no longer. Therefore, if anyone is in Christ, he is a new creation. The old has passed away; behold, the new has come. (2 Cor. 5:16–17)

The gospel changes who we are. It literally changes everything.

How the Gospel Changed My Life

The gospel changed everything for me. When God saved me as a young child, my life would never be the same. Once lost, now I'm found. Once a slave to sin, now I'm a child of God. Once living for the world, now I live for a better, bigger, eternal kingdom (Col. 1:13–14). Everything about my old life has lost its charm.

In light of eternity, it's nothing. I have a new heart, new motivations, new dreams, and keep in step with a new world (Heb. 11:16). I'm a Christian.

And like every Christian, I'm learning as I go. I still mess up and deal with mistakes and failures and frustration and pride. Being a Christian doesn't mean I'm perfect, or that I *think* I'm perfect; it means I'm striving for perfection. I'm chasing after holiness. Even though I struggle with sin, I no longer love it. My aim is to follow a new path and live for a new kingdom.

Christians who live for this new kingdom have a new King. His name is Jesus. Because of him, everything is transformed. We're now part of a counter-culture movement. We're not like the other teenagers around us. We don't conform to stereotypes. We've actually become weird in the eyes of our culture. Teen magazines are not written for us. Modern pop music is not composed for us. The latest TV lineup is not scripted for us. We're not your average teenagers anymore.

What are we? We are free. Following Jesus means we don't have to live the way our culture tells us to. We get to live in a richer and more meaningful and satisfying way every single day (Heb. 12:28–29).

We are Jesus-followers. That means we don't have to waste our lives. It means we do hard things. It means we turn our backs on what the world says is cool. It means we're members of a mission that will change everything. It means we stand out from those around us like blazing light in a pitch-black room. It means we're in a war, and we fight long and hard every day on the winning side.

Make no mistake; Jesus changes *everything*.

This is the truth I've learned: if you live for Jesus, you can't live an unchanged life. If the gospel is true, it will inescapably change every little part of us—what we do and think and say and mean, and who we hang out with and esteem and listen to and why, and how we live today and tomorrow and for all eternity. It will not be easy, safe, or always comfortable by any means. But it will be good. It will awake in you deep and unquenchable joy.

So are you ready to find out who you are? Are you ready to join a new kingdom and listen to a new battle cry? Are you ready to be considered weird by the world yet precious by your Savior? Are you ready to break free from culture's confines and discover what it means to follow Jesus every day?

Then let's get started.

• • •

Our Identity—Discussion Questions

1. How would you answer the question, "Who am I"? What are you tempted to place your identity in besides Jesus?

2. What does John 15:18–19 teach us about standing out from the world, and how does that help us overcome our fear of being different?

3. How did the gospel change your life? Write out your own testimony of how God saved you.

2

OUR STORY

I made a movie once. It was pretty awful. I was ten, and I used a long, slim Digital Blue camera I'd won from a magazine contest. I still remember editing the movie on my parents' computer and typing out the credits: *Written by Jaquelle Crowe. Filmed by Jaquelle Crowe. Starring Jaquelle Crowe.* Travis must have been busy that day because I was the only actor in the entire movie and the entire film crew. (Are you starting to get a sense of why it was so bad?)

It was called *Mystery on Warren Street* (and yes, I lived on Warren Street—What can I say? I was master of the creative title . . .), and it consisted of me stalking the empty house next door to us, making up terrible crimes that had been committed within its walls, and fantasizing about extravagant treasures buried beneath its floorboards. Then I sang some deeply moving songs about exactly how terrible the crimes and extravagant the treasures were (also written by yours truly, naturally). It was Nancy Drew meets cheesy horror flick meets Disney meets Broadway.

As childish as the movie was, I had a lot of fun making it for one simple reason: I got to invent a story and then insert myself into it. I allowed myself to step into the middle of a living and breathing adventure. What I didn't realize back then was that I was tapping into a fundamental part of being a Christian. A wonderful truth of living in God's world is that we *do* get to participate in a real-life story, God's story. This is the story that is traced through the narrative of the Bible and then leaps along history's timeline and continues into our lives today.

But what is God's story? The subtitle of this book is "How the Gospel Transforms the Teen Years." God's story is the gospel, and it is this story that transforms our lives in incredible and pervasive ways. It is this story that shapes our identity as Jesus-followers. This story is what informed Paul's whole existence and what informs ours. In that case, we ought to get to know it the best that we can.

You've probably heard that *gospel* means "good news." But this news isn't merely good in the trivial way we use the word, as in a "good movie" or a "good hamburger." This is the *best* news you will ever hear. I guarantee it. More important, God guarantees it. After all, it is his story.

My prayer for you as we reflect on this story together is that you won't let familiarity harden you to its beauty. If you're like me, you've heard it all before, maybe hundreds of times. Don't put up an emotional smokescreen, though, skimming quickly and brushing it aside as old news. Soak up the wonder with me afresh. Try to remember the first time you heard it and recapture a little of the original newness and color and shock. There is indescribable awesomeness ahead. Let's enjoy it together.

How the Story Starts

God's story starts a long, long time ago, before time even existed, in fact, before space and breath and stars, and it began with God. God, a triune Being (three in one)—Father, Spirit, and Son—is eternal (Col. 1:15–17). He never had a beginning, and he will never have an end (Rom. 1:20). It's impossible to wrap your mind entirely around that idea. He's not restricted by time, yet he created it and works within it (Titus 1:2). And thousands of years ago when nothing existed except God, he sovereignly authored a story of glorious redemption. It all started with light.

> And God said, "Let there be light," and there was light. And God saw that the light was good. And God separated the light from the darkness. God called the light Day, and the darkness he called Night. And there was evening and there was morning, the first day. (Gen. 1:3–5)

Over the course of six days, God created the entire world that we live in, and he did it with words. He made it all out of nothing, *ex nihilo* as the Latin phrase says, starting clean and empty. He made sun and sky and oceans and moon and anthills and evergreens and emeralds and doves and daffodils and cumulus clouds and lava and watermelon and wallabies. And then on the sixth day God created the pinnacle of his creation, a human. Formed from fresh dust, God fashioned the first man, Adam (Gen. 2:7), and literally breathed life into him.

Next God caused Adam to fall into a deep sleep, and he removed one of Adam's ribs and formed a woman from that rib, Eve. A woman! Don't miss the astonishment of that. Don't let Sunday school watercolors veil the sheer surprise and awe of it. First God speaks all of nature into existence, and then he makes a woman (a new gender, totally different from Adam) out of a bone he took from the man he made from dirt. That's amazing!

Adam and Eve had perfect, unspoiled fellowship with God and with each other. They were created without sin or defect, and they were given a task by God to rule the garden he had created for them, Eden (Gen. 2:15). God gave the humans vast freedom but also a single rule: do not eat of the Tree of the Knowledge of Good and Evil (Gen. 2:16–17). They had manifold freedom but one limitation. Right from the beginning of the story, God was clear: *Obey me, and you will be happy. Disobey me, and there will be terrible consequences.*

Sinclair Ferguson translates God's command like this. He said to them: "I am not asking you to do that because the tree is ugly—actually it is just as attractive as the other trees. I don't create ugly, ever! You won't be able to look at the fruit and think, *That must taste horrible*. It is a fine-looking tree. So it's simple. Trust me, obey me, and love me because of who I am and because you are enjoying what I have given to you. Trust me, obey me, and you will grow."[1] At this point, Adam and Eve obeyed their Father, and all was very good (Gen. 1:31).

Then Sin Entered the Story, and It Was Bad

But this part does not end happily ever after. Satan, a being created by God who chose to rebel against his good Maker, slithered into Eden in the form of a serpent and tempted Adam and Eve to eat from the forbidden tree. He encouraged them to doubt God's faithfulness, trustworthiness, clarity, and goodness (Gen. 3:1–5). "Did God *really* say that?" he suggested slyly. "God isn't really looking out for you. He knows that if you eat from the tree, you'll become like him. And he's so egotistical and glory hungry, he's just trying to protect himself from the power you could have. Eat that fruit, and you'll become God. No more rules. You'll be free."

As we all know, Adam and Eve believed that slick temptation and disobeyed God's command. It's hard to imagine what changed after that first bite of forbidden fruit, but it must have been a little like the power going out in the dead of winter. The warm light of God's perfect presence vanished and chill dread must have swollen inside them. Something was very wrong.

Suddenly sinful and terrified, Adam and Eve tried to hide from God, enormously ashamed. But no one hides from God. Their Maker found them and punished them. There were consequences for their sin, just like he had said. Because of this sin, this rebellion of humanity against its Maker, all of humankind was cursed (Rom. 5:18). Dutch theologian Herman Bavinck said it like this: "In Adam, we all sinned and thus sin became the fate of us all."[2] Adam and Eve and you and me and all of humanity were estranged from God and banished from Paradise. We were cursed with physical pain and death (Gen. 3:17–19) but more strikingly, with spiritual death. Paul, the masterful theologian, explains further: "Therefore, just as sin came into the world through one man, and death through sin, and so death spread to all men because all sinned" (Rom. 5:12).

Now our perfect fellowship with God was cracked, our relationship strained, and we had no way of getting ourselves back to Eden and back to our Creator. But in the midst of this catastrophic fall, there was a seed of hope. God promised a hero, someone who would come and fix what humankind had broken.

When God cursed Satan he told the snake, "I will put enmity between you and the woman, and between your offspring and her offspring; he shall bruise your head, and you shall bruise his heel" (Gen. 3:14–15). The promise was that a descendant of Eve would be born of woman and bruised by Satan but would win ultimate victory over the Serpent, crushing him. Hope was alive. And this was only the beginning of the story.

The Hero Enters the Scene

For years humanity waited for its hero to enter the world. God led his people along through all these years, multiplying their numbers, building them into a nation (called Israel), freeing them from slavery, leading them to a fruitful and lush Promised Land, punishing them when they disobeyed, and showing them mercy when they repented. Read through the Old Testament to see how God did this again and again—teaching, disciplining, and always loving his people.

He did this by setting up priests to be his people's intercessors, a bridge between the holy God and sinful man. These priests offered sacrifices on behalf of the people (due to their sin) and guided them in holiness according to God's Word. God also set up prophets to warn the people of the consequences of sin, the blessings of obedience, and the joy of trusting him. And he enthroned kings for his people, to fight their battles, provide protection, and lead with justice and wisdom.

But not one of these priests, prophets, or kings was perfect. Some were horribly evil while others struggled to do right, but they all eventually disobeyed God. They broke his law, shrank in fear, perpetuated ignorance or hatred, acted with injustice, and rebelled against God. Yet these offices whispered a constant promise: *A better Priest is coming. A better Prophet is coming. A better King is coming. The Hero who will fix everything is coming.*

And then he did, on a busy and unexpected night in Bethlehem. Who was the hero of this story? God himself. He entered his own story. And nothing would ever be the same. "And the Word became flesh and dwelt among us, and we have seen his glory, glory as of the only Son from the Father, full of grace and truth" (John 1:14).

The Creator of the universe humbled himself, took the form of man, and was miraculously born to an unassuming virgin. His name was Jesus (which means "savior"), and he came to do what we couldn't. He started by living a perfect life, never once stumbling or sinning. Never once did he pick on his siblings. Never once did he waste time. Never once did he disobey his parents. Never once did he lie or cheat on homework or complain about his chores.

As he grew up he faithfully proclaimed God's Word. Once when he was in a town called Capernaum, he was explaining Scripture in a temple, and the people were absolutely awestruck because they had never heard anybody speak with such intense and obvious authority (Mark 1:21–22). People were frequently amazed at the bold, powerful, and precise way Jesus spoke. The better Prophet was here, not just speaking the truth, but being the truth (John 14:6).

Jesus wasn't just a prophet, though. After living a perfect life, he made a sacrifice, bridging the chasm between holy God and sinful man. But instead of sacrificing an animal for sins, he sacrificed *himself* for all of God's people—past, present, and future (John 17:1–4; Rom. 5:8–10). Jesus became the Lamb of God to fix what humanity had broken. The better Priest was here.

But he wasn't put on the altar by the power of men. As a warrior he went to the cross because of his own power and his Father's desire. He went in obedience to fight the battle we couldn't, bore the wrath of God for the weight of our sins, and then claimed us for himself. The better King was definitely here.

Here's the thing, though: if Jesus simply died and stayed dead, nothing would change. He would have just been a religious prophet like so many others of his time, performing dramatic healings and miracles, claiming that he would be raised from the dead (Luke 24:7; 46) yet staying immovable in the ground.

But Jesus didn't stay dead. *Jesus is alive.* Rising by the power of God after three days, he defeated the Serpent then and there and secured the redemption of his people—us, sinful and estranged (1 Thess. 1:10). Only God could repair what we broke in Eden, and he did. When God promised a hero would come, nobody realized he was that hero.

> Since, therefore, we have now been justified by his blood, much more shall we be saved by him from the wrath of God. For if while we were enemies we were reconciled to God by the death of his Son, much more, now that we are reconciled, shall we be saved by his life. More than that, we also rejoice in God through our Lord Jesus Christ, through whom we have now received reconciliation. (Rom. 5:9–11)

And Jesus is coming again (Matt. 16:27–28). On a day that only God knows, he is returning to bring back Eden, to restore his people to a place that is, in fact, *better* than Eden—a new earth where there will be no sin, no pain, and no suffering (Rev. 21:1–5). We will exist to eternally worship God, commune with his people, and celebrate life together. We will have glorified bodies, unmarred by sin and by death.

So this story really does have a happy ending. Restoration will end the day. We're going back to Eden. Jesus wins. And that means, so do his people.

Just Why Does This Change Everything?

This is the story of the gospel. It's a breathtaking, brilliant, terrifying, glorious, almost too-good-to-be-true story. *Almost.* In every sense of the word, this story is the truest thing to touch your ears and be seen by your eyes. This news shouldn't just produce a superficial change in your life, a mere outward assent or a Facebook like. It should transform everything about how you live—how you talk and dress and think and engage with culture and who you hang out with and what you post on social media and read and find funny and watch.

The gospel is world altering and paradigm shifting. Nothing can be the same after you believe it. *Why?*

First, because it shows us that sin is very bad but grace is better. Because of sin, everybody after Adam and Eve is born imperfect. We're instinctively broken and depraved rebels against God (Rom. 3:9–12). It sounds harsh, but it's true. Nobody's born loving God. Instead, our natural inclination is to hate him. The gospel is only good news because there's bad news. That terrible news is that sin is real, and we are sinners. The punishment for our sin is death (Rom. 6:23). We rebelled against an infinitely good God, and so we bear the weight of his righteous wrath (Rom. 1:18; Col. 3:6).

Jimmy Needham paints a startling image of this. He says to picture yourself tied fast to train tracks with the massive locomotive of God's wrath thundering toward you. You're stuck. You can't escape. But here's the catch—you tied *yourself* to the train tracks.[3] In the same vein, I'm reminded of the I Am Second videos.[4] These videos are testimonies from high-profile individuals about the gospel's work in their lives. They all seem to have two things in common—they each understand that (1) they're sinners, and (2) before Jesus they were hopeless. You can't embrace salvation and the story of the gospel until you see sin for what it really is.

We were bad, and we were lost (Luke 19:10), and the weight of our sin crushed us. But when you see the horror of your own sin, you are freed to see the light of grace—like the removal of a blackout curtain on a brilliantly sunny day. What is grace? Grace is getting what we don't deserve, unmerited favor. John MacArthur says it's more than that, though. Grace, he suggests, is "not merely unmerited favor; it is favor bestowed on sinners who deserve wrath. . . . Grace is God's sovereign initiative to sinners (Eph. 1:5–6)."[5] Grace is Jesus saving us.

> For you know the grace of our Lord Jesus Christ, that though he was rich, yet for your sake he became poor, so that you by his poverty might become rich. (2 Cor. 8:9)

It took me a long time to realize that only people who know they're sinners understand grace. I've struggled with perfectionism all my life. Perfectionists have a problem with grace. That's because we believe we're above it. We deceive ourselves into thinking we deserve success. But the "failures," those people who are well aware of the fact that they're messed up, they're the fortunate ones who are humble enough to recognize grace for what it is—entirely undeserved.

God has to repeatedly kill the perfectionist in me to open my eyes to the dazzling and liberating truth of grace. This happens again and again. I burden myself with high-pressure expectations (e.g., in school, in cooking, in work, in writing), and when I fail to meet them, I punish myself. Then I nurse my bruised ego by convincing myself that if I can just *do* better and *be* better, I will be worthy.

But the destructive path of perfectionism lies in opposition to the gospel. In God's story, I am unworthy. That's where the gospel starts. I am the failure, the messed up, the imperfect, yet God saved me anyway. He saved me not because I was worthy but because *he* was worthy. And that is the truth that releases me from the bondage of works-driven perfectionism to the freedom of humble gratitude to the grace giver (Titus 3:4–8). The gospel is where perfectionism goes to die.

Second, the gospel changes our lives by teaching us that our hearts only have one Master. And so Christians aren't just Jesus-followers; they're also Jesus-worshipers. We owe God every last drop of our passion and service and devotion.

We haven't always known that, though. When we came into existence, we worshiped ourselves. Everybody's born with little, powerful thrones on their hearts that are never unoccupied. Before we were saved, we put ourselves on the throne. We were convinced that we existed for the purpose of making King (or Queen) Self happy, satisfied, and famous. But the gospel brings an explosive revolt against King Self, overthrowing him (or her) to make room for King Jesus, our new Master (Rom. 10:9).

That demands change. We must do a full throttle, 180-degree turn, must stop doing what we once did to please ourselves, and must start living in a way that pleases God. Even if that hurts our reputation. Even if that destroys our popularity. Even if that means people de-friend us. Even if we're laughed at. Even if it costs us. *Especially* if it costs us.

Here's the inevitable truth: our hearts will always find something to worship, and that will motivate how we live. We live for what we glory in, for what we worship. So what are you living for?

Ultimately the gospel teaches us that we ourselves are not worthy of worship. As nice as it might sound, we are not God. Before our salvation we were helpless, graceless, and totally incapable of saving ourselves. But Jesus wasn't. Jesus was the perfect human,

God in flesh, never doing wrong once. He deserves to be our Master and our Lord. He is the One who deserves everything. If Jesus is worthy, he must become the object of our worship. We now have the responsibility of worshipers to act in ways that bring him glory, to do things that make his name famous, to speak of his righteousness, and to live like neon signs pointing straight to him.

Our New Worldview

God's story is now our story. We live in the chapter that's unfolding today. This story changes everything. It means we have a new worldview, that is, a new way we perceive everything around us—good, evil, suffering, sin, community, beauty, shame, time, relationships. Your life is going to be different because you believe this. There's no way to get around it. If King Jesus has taken hold of your heart, your life will be a risky and unimaginably big adventure. It's all about him. Now let's live like it!

• • •

Our Story—Discussion Questions

1. How familiar are you with God's story? What can you do to avoid losing the thrill and wonder of it?

2. Define worldview. Why is having a Christian worldview so important?

3. Why is it necessary to have a biblical standard for sin? What does the world use to determine right and wrong?

3

OUR COMMUNITY

The gospel is God's story from beginning to end, and he is definitely the hero. But there's another character in his story we haven't really talked about. She's not popular or glamorous or even always lovable. She can be bitter, critical, slothful, or self-righteous. She's a damsel in some serious distress. But God loves her. He loves her so much, in fact, that he sent his Son to die for her.

Who is she?

She's the church.

Manuela and the New Idea of "Church"

My friend Manuela wasn't one much for church.[1] Her family never attended (besides a stray Easter or Christmas Eve), but she wasn't too concerned about it. I met her the summer

I was twelve when we were cabinmates at a Bible camp. As we walked up to the mess hall together the first day, questions bounced back and forth between us: "Where do you live?" "Is this your first time here?" "Are you in drama club?" But then another question popped into my head. And from there, it all went downhill.

I asked, "Where do you go to church?" She shifted awkwardly and paused for an uncomfortable length of time. I felt like I had said something wrong.

Finally, she replied, "My family doesn't really go to church. We just sort of do our own thing."

I was speechless. In my naïvety, I had never met anyone who claimed to love Jesus but ignored his church. Her idea is not unusual, though. It's actually pretty popular, especially in recent years. Kelly Bean wrote a whole book a couple of years ago called *How to Be a Christian without Going to Church: The Unofficial Guide to Alternative Forms of Christian Community*. Her thesis was this: "The great news is that it is possible to be a Christian and not *go to church* but by *being the church* remain true to the call of Christ."[2]

I don't remember how I responded to Manuela. I probably mumbled noncommittally or just replied, "Oh. I see." But I didn't see, and I still don't see.

How the Gospel Changes Our Idea of Church

The reason I don't see is because I believe that after the gospel saves us, it grabs our hands and leads us to church (Acts 2:46–47). The gospel transforms our hearts and makes us long to unite together in a community of God's people. It demonstrates to us Christ's colossal love for the church (Eph. 5:24–31) and calls us to love the church in return. It's impossible (or, at best, contradictory) to love Jesus and hate the church. After we're saved and have become part of the universal church (that is, all Christians everywhere), it is our responsibility to join a local church.

At least, that's the pattern of Scripture (Acts 2:42–47). Search through the New Testament, and try to find someone who is commended for or encouraged in not being part of a local body of believers. You can't. You won't. The Bible implies you'd be fragmented (1 Cor. 12:21–26). The gospel and church membership are inseparable. In Ephesians 3, Paul says the gospel is given for the sake of the church (Eph. 3:10), and it's our joy and privilege to know the love of Christ together with his people (Eph. 3:19–21). Stephen Nichols writes about this very thing: "When we talk about what it means to be a Christian, we have to be talking about our Christian life in the new redeemed community of the church. No one is an island."[3]

That's because the gospel is about community (Rom. 12:4–5). Jesus didn't die only for one individual; he saved an enormous group. And he saved them to join together. In 1 Corinthians 12, Paul compares the church to a body. Some of us are legs. Some of us are eyes. But when we're independent, we're useless. He writes, "God has so composed the body, giving greater honor to the part that lacked it, that there may be no division in the body, but that the members may have the same care for one another. If one member suffers, all suffer together; if one member is honored, all rejoice together" (1 Cor. 12:24–26).

Together. That's the theme word of the church. Just look at how Scripture reinforces this idea.

We worship together (Heb. 12:28).

We learn together (1 Tim. 4:13).

We fellowship together (1 John 1:7).

We serve together (Gal. 5:13).
We love together (John 15:12).
We share together (Acts 2:45).
We celebrate and suffer together (Rom. 12:14–15).
We sing together (Ps. 149:1).
We give together (2 Cor. 9:7–13).

When we join a local church, we join a family. And this family has a bond stronger and longer and greater than blood. We are bound by the gospel. We are together.

The Gospel Changes What We Do in a Church

A few years ago a *USA Today* article came out titled, "'Forget Pizza Parties,' Teens Tell Church." It quotes Thom Rainer, the then-president of Lifeway Christian Resources: "Sweet 16 is not a sweet spot for churches. It's the age teens typically drop out. A decade ago teens were coming to church youth group to play, coming for the entertainment, coming for the pizza. They're not even coming for the pizza anymore. They say, 'We don't see the church as relevant, as meeting our needs or where we need to be today.'"[4]

This article laments modern teenagers' busyness and their subsequent neglect of the church. But I see a bigger problem at play—churches are compartmentalized. Many Christian teenagers are pushed into a youth group with their own peers and age group, given pizza and games, and then sent home with no invitation or welcome into the bigger community of the church. At my old church in Texas, all the teenagers sat together during every Sunday service, never with their families, and interacted almost exclusively with each other. That's sad!

It's almost like teenaged Jesus-followers are led to believe that we're not really *part* of the church; we're just served by it.

But if our whole purpose of going to church is to get our needs met, we have a big problem. The truth is, if we're part of the body, we have a responsibility to the entire body. If teenagers love Jesus, we should be committed to his whole church. God doesn't call young people to attend as spectators; he calls us to invest.

Whether you're thirteen or nineteen or thirty-five or eighty, being a part of the church does not mean you're there only for you. If you're a Jesus-follower, it means you're there to love your church, to serve it, to worship with it, and to be accountable to it. Sure, there may be technical rules that bar teenagers from things like voting or having the official title of "member," but there are no second-class Christians and no second-class church members. Age doesn't divide. We are all the church. That means these are responsibilities we all have.

We're Called to Love the Church

I think my church is pretty great. I know I'm biased, and I know they're not perfect, but I love them. And I love them because I know them. The gospel pushes us into the arms of a family, not a skin-deep social club (Heb. 10:24–25). Good or bad, we are in this together.

Here's just one example of that. Near the end of high school, I had to take some big exams. The testing center was three hours away, and every test was complex and draining. They were a big deal. So when I passed them, my church family rejoiced with me. I had members calling and texting to congratulate me, stopping me in the foyer to ask what they were all about, and most important, praying for me.

Another example is not so happy. My mom deals with a lot of sickness. As I write this, it's early afternoon and she's resting in bed, on medication and in pain. She has been for the last three weeks. It's discouraging for her and difficult for my family. But it's in these times of unease that my church reaches out with overwhelming love and compassion. A few nights ago we got an impromptu roast beef dinner delivered to our door. We receive encouraging phone calls, texts, and emails just to "check in." People are constantly praying for us. They're always asking: "How can we help? What can we do to show our love better?"

And we're a pretty diverse group of people, a marvelous mishmash of different personalities and perspectives and ages and jobs. If it wasn't for Jesus and being a part of the church, we never would have met and never would have become so close. But our connection to Christ supersedes all other things.

That being said, loving the church is not always easy. Sometimes we hurt one another. Sometimes we say thoughtless or discouraging things. Sometimes there are conflicts. Sometimes we offend one another and sin against each other. But in spite of all this, we are still the family of God and that means we choose to pursue forgiveness, reconciliation, and peace with one another. You can't walk away from your family just because you don't feel like dealing with their problems. Families are in it for the long haul.

Loving the church means fellowshiping with it. My friend Nick says that fellowship with his church is one of the pillars of his spiritual life. That doesn't mean he's best friends with every single person there. (Introverts, rejoice!) It means he makes an effort to encourage and bless and spend time (even a little) with each person. This may mean striking up a conversation with the elderly man who sits alone. It could be asking a mom about her week. It might mean being an unexpected shoulder for someone to cry on.

The easiest way you can love the church is simply by showing up. It sounds easy, but most of us have no idea what just being there means to those around us. Your church family is genuinely encouraged by your presence. My friend Kyra told me as much. She's sixteen and a pastor's daughter in Ontario, Canada. "You hardly ever see teenagers at church who want to be there," she said. "That's why it's so important to go to church and encourage the older people in your congregation that there are still young people who care."

Teenagers add special life to a church. We bring passion and a unique perspective. We bring enthusiasm and service. We bring an eagerness to learn and a desire to grow. We bring zeal, joy, a love for justice, and deep compassion for the outcast. We are the church's future.

With the amount of popular studies in recent years about teenagers leaving the church in droves, your church must delight in your exceptionality. They probably know they aren't exactly "cool" in your peers' eyes, and that makes your attending and investing and loving so much bigger to them.

Loving the church also means praying for each other. Do you pray for your pastor? That he would have encouragement and discernment and boldness and compassion? Do you pray for your Sunday school teachers? Do you pray for the tired college students or the dad who's chronically ill or the big family that needs help? Do you pray for God to build and grow your church for his glory? Do you pray for the finances of your church? Do you pray for the missionaries your church supports? Do you pray for the toddlers and the employees and the employers and the retirees? Do you pray for spiritual growth? Do you pray for joy?

• • •

As I wrote that last paragraph, I felt a pang of conviction. Because I don't. I do pray for some of it—sometimes, usually when it affects me. But my church sends out an email with prayer requests every week, and as plain and easy as it is, I don't always pray for that list. I'm learning, though, that the church that loves one another prays for one another. Write out individual families' names and needs on note cards or make a list. Whatever you do, pray. Pray and love.

• • •

I just stopped writing and spent a few minutes praying for the needs of my church family. Perhaps you should stop reading and do likewise.

We're Called to Serve the Church

Christopher is twenty and serves his church by teaching and organizing kids' clubs and leading worship services or prayer meetings. Berea is sixteen and plays violin for worship at her church and attends the women's prayer meetings. Rachael is seventeen and sings in her church's choir, is involved in her youth group, and teaches AWANA. Seth is sixteen and serves by greeting new people and getting involved wherever he can.

These are just ordinary Jesus-followers I know who love Jesus and love the church. And their service makes total sense. If love is the foundation of our relationship with the church, a desire to serve should naturally bloom out of that.

All throughout Scripture we're called to serve those around us (1 Pet. 4:10; Gal. 5:13; Rom. 12:1–17). Serving your church looks differently depending on how big your church is, what they need and allow, and who you are and what your family

WAYS YOU CAN SERVE IN YOUR CHURCH

Care for the property or clean

Visit someone who is ill

Play an instrument in the service

Be a greeter

Teach Sunday school

Offer tech support

Write a note to encourage your pastor

Mentor or encourage younger kids

Spend time talking to an elderly member

Do free chores for older or needy members

Make birthday cards

Cook food to share

Work in the office or help with administration

Care for your siblings

needs. Like all godly action, it starts in the heart with you looking inside at your motives and desires. Acceptable service isn't just what you do; it's why and how you do it.

Then look at your gifts. We all have different ones, and different resources. My friend Kévin lives in France, and he reinforced the importance of this for me. He told me that the basis of every young Christian's service should be "pleasure in God," but that should then seamlessly flow into identifying and acting upon our specific God-given gifts. The church would fall apart if everybody wanted to serve in the exact same way. Talk to your parents or sit down with your pastor (or do both!) and look at your time and talents to figure out how you can serve.

There are mountains of ideas, but here are a few. You could mow the church lawn or help clean the building so the janitor or pastor doesn't have to. You could visit someone who's in the hospital or sick at home. You could play an instrument in a service. You could work at the sound desk or offer technical support. You could fold bulletins or volunteer in the office. What about helping out with the church's website or social media? Maybe you could teach Sunday school. You could offer to shovel an elderly member's driveway for free or babysit for the single mom so she can have an afternoon to herself. If you're creative, you could make birthday cards. If you can cook, you could bake cookies to encourage someone. Have you thought about reaching out to those younger than you and asking how their spiritual walk is going? Maybe there are children you could mentor. Another suggestion is to write a note of encouragement to your pastor. Perhaps you have a large family and the greatest service you could do is to watch your siblings for your parents.

In a nutshell, you serve by being kind to one another. Ashley is someone I know who really gets this. Sometimes she sits with other church members simply because they're sitting alone. She cares about people and thoughtfully remembers little things about them. She serves in so many small, wonderful ways that it's hard to keep count. Service doesn't have to mean singing in the spotlight or doing something showy. Sometimes it means changing a diaper or talking to a visitor or scooping up a runaway baby. Sometimes it means doing something dirty, simple, or boring in the background. And I think those are some of the most beautiful bits of service of all.

Do you remember what Jesus said in Matthew 6:1? He offered

a warning to those who only wanted to serve for public recognition and selfish gain: "Beware of practicing your righteousness before other people in order to be seen by them, for then you will have no reward from your Father who is in heaven." Instead, he said, God rewards a humble servant's hidden service (Matt. 6:4).

We're Called to Worship with the Church

As I write today, it's the 470th anniversary of Protestant Reformer Martin Luther's death. I'm reminded of these words he once said about worship, "At home, in my own house, there is no warmth or vigor in me, but in the church when the multitude is gathered together, a fire is kindled in my heart and it breaks its way through."[5] Martin Luther understood that we worship God in a special way when we're together at a local church.

I like to think that corporate worship is the closest we'll get to heaven here on earth. Think about it. In our worship services, we fellowship together with God's people, sing praise together to God, hear his Word read and taught, give, serve, and celebrate his glory together. That sounds an awful lot like heaven.

People are always quick to correct little kids' idea that heaven is just one neverending church service. Children are usually terrified of the thought. *What could be more boring?* they think. Yet while it's true that eternity won't be an everlasting church service, if our services are joy-filled community worship, shouldn't that be a glimpse of heaven? And shouldn't that make us excited? Shouldn't we be happy to praise God?

The gospel should transform our idea of Sunday morning worship from a thing of monotonous duty to one of delight. If worship is something that should exist in our lives all week (which it is), Sunday shouldn't be a chore to get out of the way.

It should be a community response to God's glory and beauty and work in our lives.

Worship doesn't come out of rote attendance, though. You may "have" to be at a service (or simply feel obligated), but your butt in a pew does not true worship make. Those of us who grew up in church wrestle with this the most, I think. We've been to a lot of services. It's been drilled into our heads that Sunday mornings arbitrarily equal worship. I've had to learn that's simply not so. It wasn't one grand breakthrough but the slow reorientation of my perspective. As I heard sermon after sermon and the truth of God's Word began to sink in, I realized that any outward acts of worship in a church service must begin in the heart. Right worship starts with right thinking.

And sometimes we have to fix our hearts. There are Sundays I come to church grumpy because I fought with Travis before breakfast, or I'm exhausted because I had a lousy sleep, or I'm discouraged because of circumstances, and the idea of worship is just words and sounds. My eyes are on me, not God, and those are the days I need a worship check.

That's when I have to get my eyes off my sin, my ingratitude, and my fakeness and fix them fast on the beauty of God. On my worst day, he is the constant, always and absolutely worthy of worship. I have to repent and get humble, recognizing that I don't deserve to worship God, don't deserve to be breathing this morning, and don't deserve to go to church. But I *get* to.

Singing hymns and listening to sermons and taking the Lord's Supper and giving offerings are all just outward acts of an inward reality—God has saved undeserving sinners for his glory. And that should result in happy worship! Going to church on Sundays purely out of duty isn't worship; it's tradition. And tradition doesn't change anybody's life.

So make your heart right for worship. Read, sing, study, and bury yourself in Scripture during the week. Try to prepare for the sermon by reading in advance the text that will be preached on Sunday. Sometimes on Saturday nights I'll listen to or watch a sermon to remind me of the joy of God's Word. Often at family devotions on Saturday, my dad will ask if anyone has any sin against another family member that needs to be dealt with. Worship happens when our hearts are right with each other.

On Sunday mornings I love to listen to music that moves my heart to reflect on God's greatness by artists like Sovereign Grace Music, Keith and Kristyn Getty, and Matt Papa. We should also pray for the service. My friend Cassie's family has a "prayer road" on the way to their church. This is an ordinary street along their route where, when they reach it, they stop talking and spend a few minutes together praying for their service. Why don't you try that?

We're Called to Hold and Be Held Accountable by the Church

We all know that sin is easy when we give in to temptation. What we don't always realize is that temptation surrounds us every single day, especially in the digital world we live in. Sin is as easy as the pressure on an "Enter" key or the click of a "Like." Sin is as easy as laughing at a gross joke or remaining silent in the face of injustice. Sin is as easy as getting a *C* when we could have gotten an *A* or shirking responsibilities with the excuse of our youth. Sin is easy, and sin is waiting for you. The apostle Peter wrote these chilling words: "Be sober-minded; be watchful. Your adversary the devil prowls around like a roaring lion, seeking someone to devour" (1 Pet. 5:8).

That's why accountability is key (James 5:19–20). Accountability is a significant component of the church, but it's also terribly misunderstood, especially by the world at large. People think accountability means the church polices people, waiting to stab a finger of gleeful judgment in their faces. Ironically, those people fail to see that accountability is actually the opposite—it's instead an outpouring of grace. It's a shimmering implication of the gospel, the church's way of saying, *Look and listen, world. We hate sin and we love holiness.* It's grown out of community and grounded in love.

For the Christian teen in a Christian family, accountability should first and foremost take place in the home. If there is unrepentant sin in my life that I'm not aware of, I know my parents will come to me before the church does. Inevitably, the church will play a bigger role in accountability for the Christian teen in an unsaved family, or the young person who is not near their family (e.g., in university or boarding school). We all need people to love us enough to guard us. Conversely, we also need to be lovingly watching out for our church family members. Accountability isn't just "old" people keeping their eyes on "young" people. It's about all of us together helping each other along in holiness.

Accountability is more than nitpicking about sin, though. It's about fostering honesty and truth and a commitment to obey Christ above all else. Accountability isn't only coming to me when I'm sinning; it's the indirect practice of pursuing holiness. When we hear gospel preaching or read the Bible or pray together or sing together or fellowship together, we are growing in holiness. This is the center and lifeblood of accountability, and thus should be taking place in the church all the time. The church just being the church is an example of accountability, since it's fundamentally about a desire to obey. Bethlehem Baptist Church wrote this about the church and accountability:

> Church membership does not involve an expectation to live perfectly. Rather, church membership is a commitment to worship and minister in a body of believers where the members covenant together to hold each other accountable to pursue obedience to what Scripture teaches.[6]

The Church Is for Our Whole Lives

One of my all-time favorite articles published on TheRebelution.com is a piece called, "The One Thing Christians Often Miss When Picking a College." If you haven't read it, you really should. Melody Zimmerman was a sophomore in college when she wrote it, and she pointed out a big problem—when Christian teenagers are looking for a university, the one thing they often miss is a church. They choose their school and only after that do they look around for a church. Or they arrive at their school and then church hop without investing. She writes, "If we are really seeking full integration into the body of Christ, involving both what we can receive and what we can offer, it seems that we should consider a church to attend when we're deciding where to go to school."[7]

I think her perspective is brilliant but also surprisingly unusual. A lot of us are at that age when we're getting a deluge of advice about college. People are giving us recommendations, we're signing up for tours and discounts, pamphlets are pouring into our mailboxes, teachers and counselors are coaching us, and our parents are helping us fill out applications. But almost nobody's talking about the importance of a local church in the search. Too often it's just on the back burner, a long afterthought. But what if we chose a college *because* of a church? What if we let a church be the deciding factor? What if we visited churches as well as colleges?

Even in Christian circles this idea is pretty radical. Why

should it be, though? You need the church to grow and mature as a Jesus-follower. If you're moving away to go to college, look for a local body of believers to join together with. Remember that whole section on accountability? If you've moved away from Mom and Dad, and you have no nearby church family, who's going to hold you accountable? It's too easy to drift toward sin in college.

Think about this now. You need a local church. You need their accountability, their love, their service, and their worship. And they need yours.

Being the Church Together

Last Sunday we had a fellowship lunch after the worship service. Heather brought her Hawaiian meatballs, Carla her cheesy casserole, Ashley her beans and rice. Crystal made a Caesar salad with teriyaki bacon, there was lasagna and three different kinds of biscuits, green bean casserole, and some sort of Indian chicken. For dessert there were chocolate-covered strawberries, my cupcakes, Heather's upside down pineapple cake, and Darlene's humongous chocolate chip cookies. But the food wasn't really that important. We were there for the people.

We sat and ate together, drinking coffee and fruit punch long after our plates were empty. We laughed and talked with each other. Then we cleaned up together. Grandpa was sweeping the floor while Dad, Travis, Alan, and Jacob closed up the tables. Joanne, Dawn, and Heather were wiping and folding tablecloths and repackaging leftovers, and Mom was washing dishes. Others were stacking chairs and taking out the garbage, while Lynnette and Willa were corralling kids and diaper bags.

It was fun. It really was. Us just doing life together. Eating is such a simple but profound part of living in God's world. And

there we all were, doing it together, and enjoying being the family of God. Our ages didn't divide us. The seniors weren't first tier Christians, while the teenagers were the bottom rung. We were all the church.

Francis Schaeffer once said something that struck me: "If the church is what it should be, young people will be there. But they will not just 'be there'—they will be there with the blowing of horns and the clashing of high-sounding cymbals, and they will come dancing with flowers in their hair."[8] The church needs young people, but young people need the church. The gospel doesn't save us so we can be loners. The gospel saved us so we can invest in the church, and it can invest in us.

I wish I could go back to that summer I met Manuela and see her again. I'd want to give her a hug and tell her as gently as possible that she's wrong. No Christian can just do their own thing. You need the church, because Jesus gave us the church. You need the church, because it's your family.

Manuela, no one is an island.

• • •

Our Community—Discussion Questions

1. Do you know what the membership process is at your church? Have you pursued baptism and church membership? (Across many orthodox Christian denominations the process is very different, so I'd encourage you to talk to your parents and pastor about it.)

2. As you think about the humble servants in your church, who comes to mind? How can you learn from watching their example or working with them?

3. Is being accountable to your church a new idea? How does it change your thinking about sin to know that the church has a responsibility to hold you accountable for it?

4

OUR SIN

Jake is seventeen and loves Jesus more than anything. Last year he started a Bible study at his school and is now playing drums on his youth group's praise team. But lately he's started to have doubts. When he was saved, he was assured that the gospel would transform him. But Jake still sees sin invading his life and has started to believe that real Christians don't struggle as much as he does. *Maybe*, he wonders, *I'm not even saved.*

Alyssa has the night all planned out. She and her best friend will borrow her parents' car (with their permission, of course), go for pizza, and then attend the movie they've wanted to see forever. But today at church her mom informs her of different plans. A missionary couple is spending one night with them, and she wants Alyssa at home to help serve. Stung with a rush of frustration, Alyssa lashes out at her mother before spinning on her heels and storming off. The couple in the pew behind her laughs it off. The man shoots an embarrassed smile at Alyssa's mom. "That's teenagers for you," he says.

Peter is thirteen and walked into church last Sunday in a great mood. Rain drummed the roof as he joined a group of men by the coffee table. An usher peered out the window and squinted. "I hate the rain." A second man agreed. "I know, right? Church attendance will be down; the building will be drafty. I bet the attic will leak too." Peter frowned. They were right. He chimed in—the weather forecast predicted rain like this for the next three days. When they all groaned, Peter did too, his good mood washed down the drain. *Miserable.*

Bianca's dad is a pastor, and she loves the God her father teaches about as passionately as he does. But two months ago, a friend from school showed her some inappropriate pictures on her phone. Bianca liked what she saw, but she tried to suppress the feeling and never told her parents. *Pornography is only a sin for guys, right?* She still didn't tell her parents when she started looking up the pictures herself. Now she's paralyzed by shame but is convinced her parents would never understand.

Dealing with Sin Today

When we're told the gospel will transform us, that's true. Following Jesus does mean everything changes. Your life gets flipped on its head and you walk in a new direction with new motives and desires—including how we view sin. We no longer love it; instead, we're supposed to hate it and fight against it (Rom. 8:13; Col. 3:5). And it's easy to hate sin when we turn on the TV and see violent lunatics or cold-blooded terrorists—or when we see public, scandalous sins splattering the front page of the newspaper. As Christians, of course we hate murder and abortion and adultery and all the other outlandish sins the world celebrates. We know we don't live for that kingdom or walk the easy road.

But as Jesus-followers, we also have a command and a responsibility to hate the smaller sins, the sins even Christians have started to expect from teenagers, the sins that have become so regular they're pushed under the carpet and practically laughed off. To do that, we first need to recognize them as sin. And this is where we often get blinded.

The man who laughed off Alyssa's frustration and venting didn't realize she had blatantly dishonored her mom. The men who complained to Peter about the weather didn't realize they were discontent with what God had given them. The church that won't talk about female lust doesn't realize they're isolating Bianca. When we're embarrassed to share the gospel we're embarrassed of Jesus. When we love to share someone's "news" we don't realize that we're gossiping. When we fudge the truth to make a story seem more exciting we don't realize that we're lying. When we're insecure we don't realize that we're ungrateful to God. When we worry about our futures we don't realize that we're choosing not to trust God.

These kinds of expected and "ordinary" sins are threatening roadblocks for the Christian. They can ease into blind spots and wedge their way into the cracks of our lives to flourish unseen and alive. They'll have poisonous effects on us if they remain unfought. That's why John Owen said, "Be killing sin or it will be killing you."[1]

We Are Saved from Sin (aka: Justification)

But the only reason we can kill sin, and the only reason we can have victory over these everyday sins is because Christ had the ultimate victory over sin. Because of him we are declared righteous in God's sight. This is called *justification*. At a single moment in time Jesus took our sin—all of it, every ugly, little speck—and the punishment we deserved—God's total and mighty wrath—and stood in our place. He was condemned instead of us, the innocent in the place of the ungodly. God then took away our guilt and made us his children. Paul told the church in Rome, "[We] are justified by his grace as a gift, through the redemption that is in Christ Jesus" (Rom. 3:24).

In his book, *Christian Beliefs*, Wayne Grudem explained justification like this: "The sins of those justified are considered forgiven because God considers their sins as belonging to Christ, and Christ already paid the penalty for those sins. But not only does God consider those sins as belonging to Christ, he also considers Christ's righteousness as belonging to us."[2]

There are two tangible (and awesome) results of justification I want to show you. The first is that there is no longer condemnation for us (Rom. 8:1). There once was a day we were condemned, doomed, sentenced to hell. It's what our sin deserved and was the appropriate punishment we warranted. But then in an extravagant display of grace, God removed his judgment from us.

In *The Pilgrim's Progress*, John Bunyan paints a real-life picture of what this looks like. He imagines those under condemnation living in a party city called the City of Destruction. It's a happening place, fast paced and reckless, but the whole place lies under the weight of coming judgment. When someone is saved, Bunyan has them immediately flee the City of Destruction. This mirrors the truth that when we're saved, condemnation is once and for all forever removed from us—or rather, we're removed from the condemnation. We've left the City of Destruction and are barred from returning. You can't *sort of* leave a city. You can't start a new path but still keep a foot in that city. Our justification is a binding and indestructible contract. There is no way in the world that Jesus-followers are going to hell.

A second benefit of justification is that there is no more guilt for us. This is a truth deeply relieving to me. I'm one of those people who holds onto guilt longer than I should, and it's an oppressive burden to bear. It feels like a backpack of rocks glued to my shoulders, dragging me down. This is why justification is such good, good news. Because Jesus took care of our sin, we are set free from guilt's burden. When we hold onto it, we actually minimize what he did on the cross and demonstrate a lack of trust in God's power to forgive. He became our sin (2 Cor. 5:21). When we say that we deserve to feel guilty, it's like we're saying that his work wasn't enough.

Granted, this doesn't mean we shouldn't feel grieved about our sin. It's healthy and holy to feel sadness over our disobedience. This sadness isn't just mushy emotionalism but genuine shame. We messed up, we did wrong, we sinned against holy God, and that *is* serious. But when our sin has been dealt with, when we've repented, we are irrevocably forgiven and no longer have to feel lasting guilt.

Wayne Grudem adds, "Christ took the place of guilt that we all deserved so that we could take the place of acceptance we all long for."[3] Justification means we are free from condemnation and guilt and now are fully, thoroughly, wonderfully, one hundred percent unconditionally accepted in God's sight as his children (Rom. 8:15). Instead of being God's enemies, we are his family. We are adopted. We are loved. We are free.

We Are Saved to Pursue Holiness (aka: Sanctification)

But even though Jesus-followers are justified, we still wrestle with sin. That's why it's hard not to get discouraged sometimes. There are moments when I feel like Jake. I look a little closer at my life, and I'm overwhelmed by how sinful I still am. That's how I felt the other day when I scrolled through my social media pages. I saw pictures, read statuses, and skimmed tweets, and slowly a prick of self-righteousness started to grow. *I* would never post or retweet that. *I* would never laugh at that video or share that song. What was wrong with them?

And then it hit me: What was wrong with *me*? My self-righteousness puffed me up with pride, hardened my heart, and had me pointing my finger at everyone else's sin instead of dealing with my own. Then I was discouraged. I'm trying to follow Jesus, but shouldn't I be better?

That's why the reality of *sanctification* is so encouraging. Sanctification refers to the process of Christians becoming more holy as the Spirit of God works in their hearts to make them more like Jesus. It's encouraging because it means that I *am* better. I'm more like Jesus today than I was five years ago. And, even better, God will continue to transform me more and more into his image for the rest of my life. I will be more like Jesus next year than I am today.

Sanctification is a life-long process, but it's a spectacular process. It's a winding road and an adventure. Every single day God is sanctifying us. As we live for him, we get to grow. It's different than justification in that, while we had no part in being justified (that was all God), we do have a part in our sanctification.

Don't mistake me—God is the one who works on our hearts to make us more like him. But we have a responsibility to pursue holiness (Rom. 8:13). Sanctification doesn't happen while we sit back and relax. Still, our work is always worth it, because as we obey, our God has promised to be with us, to help us, to mature us, and to give us lasting victory over sin.

So let's get practical. How do we pursue holiness? How do we fight sin and get victory over it? You, Jake, Bianca, Peter, Alyssa, and I need help. We're teenagers who love Jesus and want to live like him. How do we do that? Here is what I've been learning.

FIVE WAYS TO FIGHT SIN

Feed on the Word

First and most important, we need to have hearts tethered to the Word of God (John 17:17). It's impossible to know what sin is if we don't know what God says. Jesus gives us a perfect example of this when the Devil tempted him in the wilderness. "And the tempter came and said to him, 'If you are the Son of God, command these stones to become loaves of bread.' But he answered, 'It is written, "Man shall not live by bread alone, but by every word that comes from the mouth of God"'" (Matt. 4:3–4). God's Word is what we need to grow as Jesus-followers, to survive in this world, to fight temptation, and to obey our

King. It teaches us what sin is, convicts us of it, and yet also encourages us in the battle against it.

This afternoon I was meditating on Psalm 119 and thinking about the author's desperate dependency on God's Word. It was all sufficient for him. He memorized it, read it, spoke it, obeyed it, thought about it, was sustained by it, and lived and breathed it. Reading this psalm made me ache to share the psalmist's passion. But I had to remind myself that his fierce reliance on God's Word didn't strike him one day out of the blue like magic lightning. It came from soaking in the Word day in and day out.

Let's do that too. Let's get in Scripture often, every day, and let's read all of it, even the parts that seem boring or irrelevant. The more you read the Bible, the more you'll see God's holiness and your sin. It's like a mirror reflecting who you really are, revealing your true identity. It's like a magnifying glass scrutinizing your sin, making it large print before you and bringing you to conviction. And it's like a map pointing you in the right direction, showing you how to turn from error and where to go from here. God's Word rubs a yellow highlighter over our sin, but it doesn't just leave us alone after that. It sets us up for a future of fighting sin and loving God more.

Keep the Word in front of you then. An easy way to do that is to put up Bible verses around your house. When I got my first big jewelry box as a preteen, I tucked a card with Proverbs 31:30 in front of it: "Charm is deceitful, and beauty is vain, but a woman who fears the Lord is to be praised." I remember Mom writing out Ephesians 4:29 on the white board in our family dining room: "Let no corrupting talk come out of your mouths, but only such as is good for building up, as fits the occasion, that it may give grace to those who hear."

There's a reason Paul calls God's Word the "sword of the Spirit" (Eph. 6:17). It is our greatest weapon to fight sin. Reading and knowing it gives us power to see the sin in our lives, turn from temptation, choose obedience, delight ourselves in God, and steel our hearts against sin's threat.

Hate Sin

But I have a confession to make: as much as I can find sin in my life, it's tempting for me to downplay it. When I see it, I want to make it seem like it's not as bad as it really is, because I see myself as better than I actually am. I convince myself that it's not like it's a big deal, like it's a *big* sin. I mean, I didn't *kill* anyone. I just snapped at Dad. Or I just gave a second-best effort or shared an embarrassing story about that guy none of us like anyway. Come on, everyone does that. While I love to find sin in others, I tend to minimize my own sin.

That's because I fail to see the root of my sin. I don't realize that it is really no small thing. It's actually moral insurrection against my King. It's a demonstration that I don't trust, believe, or love God enough to obey him. Sin is at the root of everything bad in our lives. Every single time we sin—even if it's as small as getting impatient in the drive-thru—we are rebelling against God and disobeying a command he's given us for our good. Our hearts are pursuing something he hates and, in essence, attempting to rob him of glory.

Not only that, but it's something that has destructive consequences. We deserve hell because of this sin, because of our rebellion against a perfect and just God. Because of this sin, Jesus went to the cross.

Furthermore, our sin has real-world consequences. Our relationships start to suffer. We worry more. We pray less. Our desire to read God's Word fades. Church becomes boring. We start to feel like God is distant. Sin attempts to ruin us. That is why we should hate it.

To help us understand its severity, think about what we're really saying when we sin. At the beginning of the chapter Peter complained about the weather. Translation: "God, I don't like what you've given me, and I think I know better than you." "I worry about my future." Translation: "God, I don't trust you or believe that you're in control." You've been wasting time on social media. Translation: "My pleasure is more important than performing the tasks God has given me."

When we understand how bad sin is—*all* sin—we are better able to see its vileness and why God hates it. Because the more comfortable I am with my sin, the less like Jesus I become.

Repent (a Lot)

Even though God justified us we still sin every day, and that means we still have to repent. Oswald Chambers says that the bedrock of Christianity is repentance. Burk Parsons says that there's no such thing as an unrepentant Christian. Repentance is needed for us to grow as Jesus-followers.

The first step in repentance is finding the sin in our lives and recognizing it as sin. This happened for me with insecurity. I have been insecure as long as I can remember. When I was younger I decided that I didn't like my ears. They were too big and therefore must never be shown. I wouldn't style my hair in ballerina buns or tuck it behind my ears. It was quite the travesty when I got the role of a cheerleader in my sixth grade church musical and I was required to have a high ponytail. The thought that I would have to stand in front of the entire congregation with my ginormous ears flapping in the fan breeze was horrifying.

Eventually I got over my ears. But insecurity still remained a common narrative woven throughout my life. I came to believe it was normal. Every teenager dealt with it, so it had to be okay. Sure, it felt horrible, but I never realized that those beliefs of inferiority were direct beliefs of ingratitude to God. I was discontent with how God had made me—he crafted these ears and this body and this brain of mine. As I read God's Word and heard godly teachers apply it, I realized that I was disobeying my Maker. Instead of contentment, I was consumed with the pride of insecurity.

My repentance involved actively turning away from this specific sin, confessing to God that I had broken his law, that I had been ungrateful, and that I had been dissatisfied with him. Then I asked for his forgiveness. What was so glorious is that I got it. When we acknowledge that God has the authority to forgive our sin, he will (1 John 1:9).

But I still get insecure, and so I need to keep repenting. Repentance is ongoing, an everyday thing—almost an every prayer thing. As much as we mess up, we need to repent and be truly sorry. What does that look like? Repentance is less about the individual prayers and what you say and more about the heart attitude—not that the words aren't important, though. We should be able to articulate how we sinned and ask for forgiveness. But God is not looking for us just to say a magic prayer. He's looking for authentic, heart-deep shame over and hatred for our sin.

I've never seen anybody take repentance as seriously as the Puritans. In a book of prayers called *The Valley of Vision*, there is a whole section of their prayers of confession and repentance (under the solemn heading of "Penitence and Deprecation"). These are written by men who were struck by a deep-seated revulsion of their sin and a twin realization of their helplessness and dependency upon God.

These men prayed things like, "Eternal Father, Thou art good beyond all thought, but I am vile, wretched, miserable, blind."[4]

They confessed, "O Lord, no day of my life has passed that has not proved me guilty in thy sight."[5] They said, "Low as I am as a creature, I am lower as a sinner, I have trampled thy law times without number; sin's deformity is stamped upon me, darkens my brow, touches me with corruptions."[6] And as much as they understood their sinfulness and despised it, they wanted to pursue holiness anew. "Lord Jesus, give me a deeper repentance, a horror of sin, a dread of its approach."[7] Could that be said of you and me?

Be Accountable to People Who Love You

In his wisdom, God has given us people to help us fight against sin. We need churches to provide pastors and teachers and mentors to point us to Scripture and help us, like rehab centers for recovering sinners. We need accountability partners. We especially need our parents to hold us accountable. And to do that, we need to talk to them about our sin and confess it. Remember Bianca? She's dealing with pornography alone, eaten up with guilt but too ashamed to tell anyone. Her first step to living a guilt-free life is to go to God. Then she needs to go to her parents.

My mom and I meet once a week. Sometimes we read a book together and discuss it at these meetings, sometimes not. They are essentially opportunities for accountability. We talk about life, what I'm struggling with, what I'm encouraged by. Without fail she always asks me how my devotions and prayer life are going. Often she asks me one-line questions to probe into how I'm really doing—for example, "What makes you happy right now?"; "What makes you sad?"; "What makes you angry?" She routinely asks me if there's sin I'm struggling with, and there are weeks she offers me counsel on sin she sees in my life.

Accountability means having someone love you enough to help you fight against sin. In a lot of cases that will be your parents, but it might not be. It might be an older member from your church or your pastor or a teacher. Accountability to them means having the kind of long and uncomfortable talks the world makes fun of. It means being open and vulnerable. It means awkwardness, but it also means freedom.

Pursuing holiness without accountability is like walking down a narrow road sandwiched between two deep ditches. It would be impossibly easy to fall astray without the guidance of accountability's guardrails.

Be Humble

Jon Bloom wrote that the "greatest enemy of our souls is the pathologically selfish pride at the core of our fallen nature."[8] If pride is at the root of all sin, humility must be the fundamental antidote. Christians hear a lot about humility, but we don't spend a whole lot of time talking about what it actually looks like. What does being humble mean in the real world?

Humility is understanding our littleness and God's bigness. Jonathan Edwards once said, "The saints in glory are so much employed in praise, because they are perfect in humility, and have so great a sense of the infinite distance between them and God."[9] There's no three quick steps or six fast tips to get it. The Bible presents it as a lifelong pursuit. It's more than self-deprecation or a few nice actions; it's a pervasive heart attitude. Peter tells young people to clothe ourselves with humility, "for God opposes the proud but gives grace to the humble" (1 Pet. 5:5).

Humility is surrendering the daily acts of pride in our lives—the pity parties, the comparison, seeking attention, the flattery, the people pleasing. It's choosing to measure ourselves up to God's standards (instead of peoples') and then embracing how short we fall. When we recognize our human weakness, we're set free to be used by God in the most powerful ways. Paul got this, which is why he could say, "When I am weak, then I am strong" (2 Cor. 12:10).

Humility is the intentional recognition that glorifying God is more important and joy-inducing than glorifying myself. It's also the accompanying action that reflects the praise back to him. It's not merely thinking a certain way; it's living like it.

Humility results in gratitude. We reject our natural dissatisfaction with circumstances and embrace a heart that thanks God for what he's given us. Humility results in words spoken kindly. Instead of anger, we know we are undeserving of grace and so choose to extend charity to others in our speech. Humility results in peace. We know that we're not in control, and so we push away worry and anxiety and thrust everything at God's feet. Humility always results in prayer. We know that we can do nothing in our own power and strength, and so we rely on God.

Following Jesus in humility means stepping out of the spotlight and redirecting it to the One who deserves it. And that is the greatest sin killer of all.

You Are Not Alone

Yet even as we pursue holiness, teenagers who follow Jesus can still feel like they're battling alone. We're told the gospel will change our lives, but we still fight against sin every day. It's tempting to feel isolated and lonely, like we're the only Christian teenagers in the whole world trying to obey him. But there is a truth bursting with hope for us today: God is with us.

The Holy Spirit dwells inside us and is the One who changes our hearts, making us desire to feed on God's Word more, hate sin more, repent more, be held accountable more, and grow humbler. As we pursue holiness, the Spirit is the one who grants us that holiness. It comes little by little, day by day, and it can sometimes feel like slow going—but take heart, *it is going*.

The End of the Stories

While we're at the end of this chapter, we're only at the beginning of our stories. Justification is where it starts, but sanctification is a journey we're on for the rest of our lives. We—sinful, rebellious people—have been adopted into the God of the universe's family. And he—the sovereign Creator who spoke this world into existence—is transforming us. He is working in our hearts every single day. He worked yesterday. He is working today. He will work tomorrow. Because the Son of God became like us and died for us, we can become like him. We can have victory over our sin.

The gospel changes everything in our lives. Jake now knows he's justified and is in awe that God is working in him to make him more like Jesus. Alyssa has realized that, despite the difficulty of honoring her parents with joy, God has commanded it of her and he will help her do it. Peter walked into church this Sunday, and it was raining again—but instead of complaining, he chose to express gratitude to God. Bianca has finally realized how pornography is hurting her heart and, after confessing her lust to God, told her parents everything. Now they're walking through the next steps for how she can pursue holiness.

God is working in the lives of the Jakes, the Alyssas, the Peters, and the Biancas. He's working in my life. And he's working in yours. If you are saved, you will grow. The God of heaven and earth has promised that, and he has promised to help you every step of the way. And this God doesn't break his promises.

• • •

Our Sin—Discussion Questions

1. What are some "ordinary" or "expected" sins you struggle with, and what steps can you take to root them out?

2. Who do you have (or who could you have) in your life who will hold you accountable? What fears do you have about being held accountable? What encourages you about being held accountable?

3. What part does gratitude play in the fight against sin?

5

OUR DISCIPLINES

Let's pretend there are two teachers at your school. I'll call one Miss Rose. The other will be Mr. Smith. Miss Rose has known you since you were born and is part cheerleader and part grandma to you. She's a gracious grader, but she genuinely wants you to learn, and invests hours into teaching you everything you need (and want) to know. Mr. Smith, on the other hand, hates teaching you. You annoy him by breathing. He's constantly cranky, unfairly critical, and irrationally harsh. His class is miserable.

Now let's pretend that both Miss Rose and Mr. Smith assign you a difficult paper on an interesting subject. Miss Rose is thrilled to help you. She's arranged a special field trip and offered you a mountain of rewards. Mr. Smith is his usual grumpy, detached self. "I don't care about you or the paper," he informs you, "but if you want a good grade, get it done and make it good."

How you view the two papers will be dramatically different. You still have to do both of them, but writing for Miss Rose will be a joy. She loves you and is leading you to success. Not so with Mr. Smith. Writing for him is a bitter and begrudging duty; there's zero delight. It's performance driven, and your only motivation is to pass the course and get on with life.

This illustration teaches us a lot about the theme of this chapter—spiritual disciplines. What we'll study in the pages ahead are certain activities Jesus-followers do as students of God, not to be saved, not to pass a course, but to reflect their love for God. They do them to obey. They do them to grow in their faith. And they do them out of joy. Because their God loves them with an everlasting love. Because their God is worthy of everything. Because their God is their Father, their friend, and their comforter. Because their God is good, and he cares for them.

What Are Spiritual Disciplines?

But first, let me define what I mean by *spiritual disciplines*. I get this phrasing from 1 Timothy 4:7–8: "Discipline yourself for the purpose of godliness; for bodily discipline is only of little profit, but godliness is profitable for all things, since it holds promise for the present life and also for the life to come" (NASB).

In this passage God calls young Timothy (and by extension, every Christian) to discipline himself in godliness. How? By intentional and committed biblical actions that correct or train us in Christlikeness—i.e., disciplines. Donald Whitney wrote a wonderful book on this subject (called *Spiritual Disciplines for the Christian Life*). He defines spiritual disciplines as "those practices found in Scripture that promote spiritual growth among believers in the gospel of Jesus Christ. They are habits of devotion, habits of experiential Christianity that have been practiced by God's people since biblical times."[1]

This subject is a natural leap from the previous chapter. Chapter 4 explored the things Christians are told *not* to do (i.e., sin). This chapter invites us into the things Christians are *told* to do (i.e., disciplines). The gospel leads us away from sin and right into the arms of joyous discipline.

When you read through the Bible, you'll see more than a dozen spiritual disciplines played out in principle or practice, but I want to focus in on just four. These are four disciplines every Christian must be pursuing—Scripture reading, memorization, prayer, and evangelism.[2]

Do Teenagers Have to Practice the Disciplines?

Oddly enough, some people believe that young Christians don't need to practice the disciplines. They assume we can start them when we're older. But that idea is found nowhere in the Bible. In fact, it's quite contrary to God's expectations laid out in his Word. He doesn't have one set of commands for the "old" and one for the "young." All Christians—toddlers, tweens, teens, twentysomethings, thirtysomethings, fifty-, sixty-, seventy-, hundredsomethings—all of us, are called to obey God consistently and happily.

Plus, practicing these disciplines while we're teenagers is actually an advantage. We're setting ourselves up for a life of sustained gospel growth. My friend Isabelle recently reminded me of this. She told me, "There is no, 'Ok, adult Christians, do this, but you teenagers are off the hook.' [The disciplines apply] to every single person, regardless of their age. Furthermore, it's of great benefit to us to do these disciplines while we are younger, as our brains are more malleable and able to retain information. If a tree has a certain bent when it is young, it will completely lean that way when it is old. If we form these good habits and fill our mind with the Word when we are young, God can use it powerfully for the rest of our lives."

Getting at the Heart of Spiritual Disciplines

Still, before we can look closer at how to practice the spiritual disciplines as teenagers we have to understand something very important—*why* we practice them. We don't do them to be saved; we do them because we *are* saved. We don't do them to earn gold stars in God's gradebook; we do them to obey his clear commands. We don't do them just because we *have* to. That's what motivated students in Mr. Smith's class. It was all duty and frustration-fueled drudgery.

We're in Miss Rose's class now. We do them because we *get* to. We practice the spiritual disciplines because we are motivated by abundant affection for Christ and a thriving desire to grow in him. We do them because of the gospel.

Here's the thing about disciplines—to obey God in the way he commands, we need to have the right motivation. We can read our Bibles for two hours every day and still not be honoring God through that. If our hearts are motivated by the wrong thing, the practice is empty. If our hearts are not relying fully on Christ, it's futile.

Yet let me be clear: that doesn't mean we should only practice the disciplines if we feel like it. God doesn't just suggest it; in his Word he commands it. We must obey, but the point is that we should obey cheerfully. The heart of spiritual disciplines is gospel joy, and it is this joy that fuels every Christian—even and especially the young ones—to read our Bibles, memorize them, pray, and evangelize.

Reading God's Word

Dad often says that if God called us on the phone and told us he had a message for us, we would go wild for a chance to talk to him. Of course we would. That would be an incalculably precious gift, practically inconceivable. But Dad always adds, God *has* done that. Do you want to hear God speak to you? Open the Bible.

Yet we have to discipline ourselves to regularly, daily read God's Word. We're tempted by a myriad of things to keep us away—busyness, boredom, sleepiness, social media, etc. But God blesses us and speaks to us through the Bible. Shouldn't our love for him drive us to his Word?

The writer of Psalm 119 had a kind of explosive and intense love for Scripture that may seem foreign to us (remember his example in the previous chapter?). Just read these words and let them sink in:

> Your testimonies are wonderful;
>   therefore my soul keeps them.
> The unfolding of your words gives light;
>   it imparts understanding to the simple.
> I open my mouth and pant,
>   because I long for your commandments.
>   (Ps. 119:129–131)

How do we steal this same love for God's Word? First, we need to read it more, often, every day, and we need to read all of it. The psalmist loved the Word because he knew it (Ps. 119:15–16). A modern help we have for that is a reading plan. This is a struc-

Bible Reading Plans to Get Started	
Legacy Reading Plan	http://www.equip.org/PDF/LEGACY_READING_PLAN.pdf
Robert Murray M'Cheyne Reading Plan	http://www.mcheyne.info/calendar.pdf
Bible Reading Plan for Shirkers and Slackers	http://www.ransomfellowship.org/publications/notes_biblereadingprogram.pdf
The Bible-Eater Plan	https://blogs.thegospelcoalition.org/tgc/files/2012/12/BibleEaterTrentHunter-3.pdf
Two-Year Bible Reading Plan by Stephen Witmer	https://blogs.thegospelcoalition.org/tgc/files/2010/12/TGC-Two-Year-Bible-Reading-Plan1.pdf
Discipleship Journal Bible Reading Plan	http://www.calvarysac.org/images/docs/reading_plans/discipleship.pdf

tured schedule that gives you a portion of Scripture to read every day. I start a plan every January where I read through the entire Bible in one year. It takes care of the hardest part of reading—where to begin. As challenging as this seems, it will most likely take you less than ten minutes every day.[3] That's really not much.

There are lots of different plans out there. There's one where you read a passage from the Old Testament and a passage from the New Testament every day. There's also a four-place plan, where you read from a historical book, the Psalms, a gospel, and an epistle at the same time (this is similar to the M'Cheyne Bible Reading Plan). There's the Legacy Readers Plan which goes by months instead of days (e.g., you're told to read Genesis and Exodus in January). Travis did a three-year Bible reading plan his first time. At the end of the day, though, it's not really about the plan, or even whether you have a plan. It's about disciplining yourself to consistently read God's Word.

But it's not just about getting it read. The discipline is not training our eyes to run over words, closing the book, and forgetting everything we just read. A central part of reading Scripture is *meditation*. This is not a mystical or mushy New Age concept. This is a biblical practice. We see it right in Psalm 119: "I will meditate on your precepts and fix my eyes on your ways" (v. 15). It's taking God's Word and thoughtfully reflecting on it. I try to pick a few verses from my daily Bible reading and think about the context, the meaning, and the application. I think about what it teaches me about God's character and his plan of salvation. I just let it roll around in my mind.

David Mathis, who also wrote an excellent book on spiritual disciplines (called *Habits of Grace*), says this:

> For the Christian, meditation means having "the word of Christ dwell in you richly" (Col. 3:16). It is not, like secular meditation, "doing nothing and being tuned in to your own mind at the same time," but it is feeding our minds on the words of God and digesting them slowly, savoring the texture, enjoying the juices, cherishing the flavor of such rich fare.[4]

God called his servant Joshua to this kind of powerful, engaged reflection in Joshua 1:8. It was a scary point in Joshua's life. He had taken over leadership of Israel after Moses's death and God repeatedly told him to "be strong and courageous" (Josh. 1:9). But how could Joshua do that? God said: "This Book of the Law shall not depart from your mouth, but you shall meditate on it day and night, so that you may be careful to do according to all that is written in it. For then you will make your way prosperous, and then you will have good success" (Josh. 1:8).

Joshua's courage and success came from knowing God intimately through meditating on his Word. If you want that, invest yourself in Scripture. Journal about it. Take notes. Study it. Think about it every day. Relish it. Enjoy it. Then you can say with the psalmist, "In the way of your testimonies I delight as much as in all riches. I will meditate on your precepts and fix my eyes on your ways. I will delight in your statutes; I will not forget your word" (Ps. 119:14–16).

Memorizing God's Word

If we're delighting in God through reading and meditating on his Word, it only makes sense that we should memorize it too. Unfortunately, we often don't. As many excuses as we have for not reading the Bible, we have double for not memorizing it—no time, too hard, bad memory, don't know where to start, etc.

If memorizing Scripture is fueled by a love for Christ, though, these duty-driven excuses should melt away. We should *want* to think about the Bible so much that we commit it to memory. Our friend from Psalm 119 sure thought so. "With my whole heart I seek you; let me not wander from your commandments! I have stored up your word in my heart, that I might not sin against you" (Ps. 119:10–11).

I've learned this firsthand. When I was thirteen, Dad told me he had read an article. (Conversations that start like this are some of my favorites.) "It's about memorizing Scripture," he said. "This guy suggests you consider memorizing whole books of the Bible. And he has a method to do it."

I like a good challenge, and so I read the article too, albeit with some qualms. It was by Dr. Andrew Davis, titled "An Approach to Extended Memorization of Scripture."[5] In it he lays out a methodical, slow, and patient approach to memorizing a big chunk of Scripture. It's usable, practical, understandable, and allows for long-term retention and easy verse location.

I told Dad, "Let's do it." But I had one condition—I got to pick the book. He agreed, and I chose Colossians, a ninety-five-verse, four-chapter book packed full of glorious truth and

TIPS FOR MEMORIZING SCRIPTURE

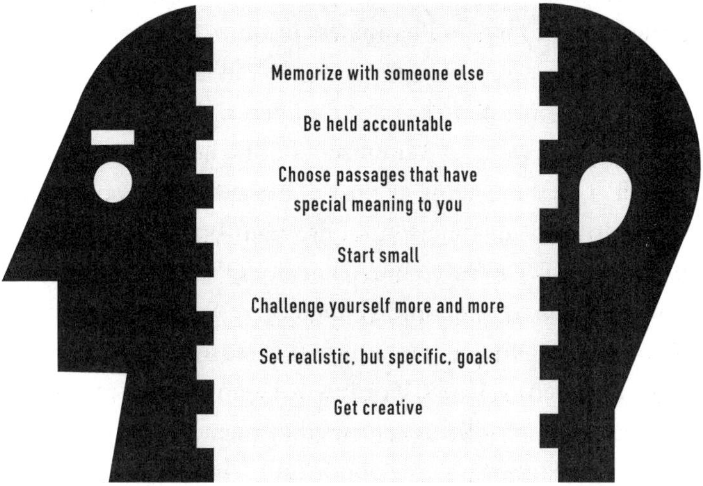

everyday wisdom. We memorized it in just over four months. It was so doable that three months later we decided to memorize another book. This time was Dad's choice, and he picked Habakkuk, a three-chapter minor prophet about a guy who wrestles with God's sovereignty in the midst of evil, eventually coming away with a renewed trust in God. It's beautiful.

We had seven chapters of God's Word hidden in our hearts, but we were still talking about memorizing another book. Andrew Davis had revolutionized our concept of Scripture memory. Every day we memorized one new verse and reviewed all the others. It wasn't impossible. We were back to my choice in picking a book now, so I suggested Romans. Dad laughed. He thought I was joking.

I wasn't.

It took us under a year to memorize Romans. Now we try to recite or read these three books at least once a month, every month. Our memories aren't flawless, but God's Word is in there, a solace in times of grief, sharp conviction in times of sin, hope in times of fear, and happiness in times of emptiness.

I tell you this to encourage you—you can memorize Scripture too. If I can, you can. It has been a liberating practice for Dad and me. I don't want to minimize its difficulty, but its rewards outweigh everything going against it. Besides, as a teenager, you have an intrinsic advantage built into your brain—it is easier to memorize when you're young. That doesn't mean it's *easy*, or that older Christians shouldn't memorize Scripture. It means that it is easi*er*, and you should use this season God has you in to learn as much of God's Word as you can. I often meet older Christians who can still recite verses they memorized as teenagers and who bemoan wasting the opportunity they had to memorize so much more. Hear their cry. Don't waste this season.

A personal recommendation is to partner with someone for accountability—and because, honestly, it's just more fun. Dad and I would invent raps or rhymes or acronyms for some verses. We would help each other along, quiz each other, and dole out tough love or motivation when the other needed it most. Ask your mom or dad or a friend or a mentor if they would be your memory partner. You don't need a partner to memorize Scripture, though. My friend Donna memorized the book of Romans all on her own, pushing through by diligent perseverance and prayer. While memorization is certainly harder for some people than others, I believe anyone can memorize.

If the idea of memorizing an entire book scares you (which, trust me, I get), start smaller. Check out Fighter Verses, a resource created by Desiring God to compile shorter sections of Scripture for memorization. Or choose one of your favorite passages from God's Word and start there. Then utilize resources.

Resources for Scripture Memory

An Approach to Extended Memorization of Scripture by Andrew Davis	
Fighter Verses	desiringGod.org
The Verses Project	theversesproject.com
Seeds Family Worship	seedsfamilyworship.com
Typographic Verses	typographicverses.com
Memorize Now	memorizenow.com

If you're musically inclined, look into The Verses Project or Seeds Family Worship. If you don't know where to start and are eager for a challenge, read Dr. Davis's article and pick a book of the Bible. For the visual learners out there, there's Typographic Verses, a website that has copies of gorgeously illustrated verses. Memorize Now is a customizable flash card system. There is truly a wealth of resources for every kind of learner.

The work, the discipline, is worth it. I promise. These are God's infallible, priceless, precious, very breathed words (2 Tim. 3:16). They give life. They reap joy. And they help us in our other disciplines—especially in our prayer life.

Praying

Only recently have I come to understand that reading, meditating, and memorizing should flow seamlessly into prayer. Instead of divorcing the disciplines from each other, connecting them like dots makes more sense. The Puritan Thomas Manton does that when he says: "The word feedeth meditation, and meditation feedeth prayer. . . . [M]editation must follow hearing and precede prayer. . . . What we take in by the word we digest by meditation and let out by prayer."[6] When we read God's Word, we should be drawn into prayer—and to a particular kind of Scripture-directed, meditation-fed prayer.

This has been a game changer for my daily devotions. Instead of thinking I have to switch gears when I close my Bible and move to prayer, I think about what I've read. I praise God for how he worked or is glorified in the text. I ask forgiveness for the sin I'm convicted of in the text. I pray for specific people and situations the text sparks in my mind. I pray for other things too, but fundamentally my engagement with God's Word leads organically to prayer.

The discipline of prayer isn't merely regulated to one ten-minute block a day, though. We're called by Paul to "pray without ceasing" (1 Thess. 5:17). This happens when our love for and trust in God ties us to him throughout the day. Our conversation with him happens in the car, on the way to school, at school, during lunch and work and homework and chores—and it doesn't have to stop with a formal "amen." Prayer should be a constant dependence on him and natural, persistent posture of us coming to him again and again.

I struggle with this. A reason for that struggle is the temptation to believe prayer is a very ordinary thing. I've grown up surrounded by praying people, and I used to find it very common. Talking to God happened all the time—before meals, in family worship, at church—and it just seemed as if it wasn't a big deal. But I need to remind myself repeatedly of an awesome truth: *prayer is a privilege*. Prayer is communication between sinful man and holy God only made possible by the work of Jesus as our Sacrifice and Intercessor. It's humans with direct access to the divine. That's miraculous. I don't care how often you do that—every single time, that's amazing.

The start of praying more is getting a sense of what prayer really is. Spend some time in Scripture and observe how people communicated with God. It left them wonderstruck and prostrate. It was gloriously good but also serious and solemn and never taken lightly. Yet almost paradoxically, it's something we're told to do all the time, because Jesus gave us direct access to God. That's shocking. That's awesome.

Another facet of disciplining ourselves in prayer is to pray with others. My family prays together every night. Mom and I have a special time of prayer together at least once a week. It can be transformative. I remember one night when Dad was out of town, and just Travis, Mom, and I were doing family devotions together. Instead of having a regular prayer time, Travis brought his private prayer list and prayed through it with us. Listening to him come to our God with worship and humble requests, to hear him pray for me and for the things going on in my life, to unite our hearts with his before God was deeply bolstering to my own faith.

You can also read books by godly people who apply Scripture's wisdom about prayer in practical ways. Two that have helped me are *Praying Backwards* by Bryan Chappell and *A Praying Life* by Paul Miller. Or you could read books of actual prayers. My favorite is *The Valley of Vision* (see page 73). While these books can be instrumental in helping us better practice this discipline, let me give you one caution (sprouted from unfortunate personal experience): don't spend more time *reading* about prayer than actually *praying*. Christ has made a way for you to talk to the God of the universe. Don't brush that aside. Really pray.

Evangelizing

On the Saturday before Christmas last year, I found myself downtown. But I wasn't shopping. Along with a small group of other Christians, I was handing out gospel tracts. It was a sunny but bitterly cold Canadian afternoon, and we were wrapped in layers and layers of warm clothes, our noses and hands red and tingly. But people streamed past us, and we kindly and calmly handed out boxes of Christmas-themed tracts. Some people said, "No thanks," others threw them in the garbage, some laughed at us, others got annoyed, but the gospel made its way into hundreds of hands.

One of my friends who had joined us was a new Christian, and she loved this time. While initially nervous, she began to fall into a rhythm and steadily grew bolder and more passionate. When we prepared to leave, she was contagiously happy. "There's one thing I don't understand," she told me as we packed up our things and headed to the cars. "Why don't more people do this? Why don't people tell others about Jesus? It's so fun!"

Fun is not the first word most Christians would use to describe evangelism. *Scary*, probably. *Hard*, definitely. But fun? I don't think so. Yet this Christian had experienced one of her first tastes of this discipline and was already enjoying its powerful fruit—joy.

But let's back up a minute. What exactly is evangelism? Is it handing out tracts on a street corner? Is it preaching in the open air? Or can it just be living a certain way without ever speaking about Jesus? Dr. Whitney has a wise and fairly simple answer. He writes that it's "communicating the gospel. Anyone who faithfully relates the essential elements of God's salvation through Jesus Christ is evangelizing. This is true whether your words are spoken, written, or recorded, and whether they are delivered to one person or to a crowd."[7]

Evangelism is verbally sharing the gospel. That might be with a friend over coffee. It might be on your blog. It might be at an outreach with your church. It might be with a family member on the phone. It might be with a stranger on an airplane. It might be with your teacher through an assignment. It might be with your coworker during break time. It might be on social media. It might be with your sibling on a family vacation. It begins with living the gospel and ends with speaking it.

But what about all the challenges? The fear, the difficulty, the risk of rejection, the possibility of strained relationships? The answer is yes. Yes, those things are real, and yes, they have to be dealt with, but evangelism is not a take-it-or-leave-it slice of Christianity. Jesus commands all believers to "go into all the world and proclaim the gospel to the whole creation" (Mark 16:15). Young people aren't excused from this call because of age or inexperience. If we believe the gospel, we can put it into words. And if we can put the gospel into words, we can share those words with someone else. Friend, we have to. Aren't souls worth more than comfort?

Evangelism is obedience, but it's also a visible act of humility. It takes our eyes off of ourselves and fixes them on God's bigger story for the world. The gospel does not start and end with us. From first to last, it's about him and his plan to save people from every tribe and nation and tongue. Yet in his almost incomprehensible mercy, he has given us a role and responsibility in that global plan—to be his messengers.

We're called to be "ambassadors" for the gospel, because the primary way God saves people is through the witness and testimony of Christians (Rom. 10:14–17). That's how he saved me, through my parents' faithful evangelism. And my parents weren't some kind of old and hyperspiritual super-Christians. They were just two Jesus-followers in their twenties sharing the gospel with their little ones.

As teenagers, we have a unique opportunity for evangelism

with the people we know. We have teammates and coworkers, teachers and classmates, fellow club members and online friends. We know people our pastors or parents will never have the chance to share the gospel with. Those individuals are our God-given gospel windows. We don't want to miss them.

That's local evangelism, something we're all called to. There's another kind of evangelism, though, global evangelism—or missions. This is going somewhere else to share the gospel and make disciples, usually somewhere foreign. Not everyone is called to be a missionary, but some undoubtedly are. You might be. I would encourage you to talk to your parents or pastor about it, especially if you feel led to serve in this area. Still, whether you go overseas or not, evangelism is a pressing demand for any and every Christian. Remember, it's a command.

Before you get discouraged by the growing burden, let's connect the disciplines' dots again. Remember how I said that the spiritual disciplines are tied to each other? This is blatantly true of evangelism and prayer. God is the One who saves, so the discipline of evangelism should actually start on our knees. It should start with us praying, praising, begging God to save, asking, longing (and then looking) for opportunities to share the gospel.

Don't put the pressure on you. *God* changes hearts. *He* works through our mistakes and our blunders. *He* uses us for his glory and is pleased by our efforts. *He* is the Savior. After all, it is his story.

It's Time to Enjoy Miss Rose's Class

And it is this story, the gospel, that motivates our practice of the spiritual disciplines. We love Jesus, so we read his Word and meditate on it and memorize it and pray it and share it with others. Like students in Miss Rose's class, we enjoy our assignment because we enjoy Miss Rose.

But we're not talking about a fictitious teacher here. We are talking about the all-powerful and infinitely good Savior of the world. This Savior loves us deeply and fantastically. He's not just an attentive teacher cheering us on, but a brother, friend, and King who has our best interests, needs, and desires at heart and whose Spirit is at work within us. He loves our service to him. He blesses us for our service to him. He is our motivation.

And that's what fuels our reading, our memorizing, our praying, and our evangelizing: Jesus.

• • •

Our Disciplines—Discussion Questions

1. What disciplines do you find the most difficult to cultivate? Why do you think that is?

2. Think of some of the godliest people you know—either personally or throughout history. What priority did they make cultivating spiritual disciplines? What steps can you take today to follow their example?

3. Why is it so important to remember the heart of spiritual disciplines?

6

OUR GROWTH

Killing houseplants runs in my family. My mom is the master plant murderer, at least when she's indoors. Give her a garden outside and plants have a 99 percent better rate of survival. When we lived in British Columbia she had quite a thriving garden in our backyard. She even grew pumpkins one year. But, put the lady in charge of a pot on the kitchen windowsill, and it's *planticide*.

I recently discovered that she's passed along this evil power to me. Last month I dog-sat for my grandparents, and Grandpa left me a list of instructions for Kit, his puppy. "Oh yeah," he added as an afterthought, "and maybe you could keep an eye on that plant while you're here." They came home three weeks later to a happy, healthy Kit. I had fed her full, kept her water bowl brimming, taken her on long walks, and given her heaps of treats and attention. The plant, on the other hand, was on death's doorstep.

I tell you about this like it's some sort of magical power (evil curse?) Mom and I have. Like we do everything we can to keep a plant alive (give it sunlight, water it every day, mash in some Miracle-Gro, sing to it), yet it somehow mysteriously still dies. But the truth is we don't do all that. The plant dies purely because we're inattentive. We just don't care about its health and growth, and so we forget to put in the persistent hard work of tending it.

Caring for plants reminds me that growth takes a lot of work. It demands time and thought and pruning and feeding and watering and weeding and strategizing and sunshine. If even one of those demands flounders or fails, the plant will most certainly die. Growing a plant takes real, regular work.

As does growing more like Jesus.

Grow Up or Die

Growth is a necessary survival function for all living things. If a flower grows, it's alive. If it stops (or never starts), it withers and dies. That's basic biology. The same is true for Christians. When the gospel saved us, it made us alive in Christ, breathing life into our dead hearts (Col. 2:13). We became wide awake and hungry spiritual newborns, thirsty sprouts, our eyes freshly opened to the world. And immediately, we started growing.

That growth will never stop. It's a sign of spiritual life. We will inescapably keep learning and growing and growing and learning, on and on, forever. A Christian that doesn't grow is an oxymoron. It doesn't exist. To follow Christ is to be a lifelong learner. We grow because we're alive.

Discernment = Growth

But we cannot grow without discernment. These two things are inextricably bound together. What is discernment? It's simply the ability to define and act upon the difference between right and wrong, or, as C. H. Spurgeon so famously said, between "right and almost-right." It's looking out over the landscape of our lives; examining everything we encounter; and judging between good and bad, between biblical and false doctrine, between edifying and harmful entertainment, between holiness and sin. In 1 Thessalonians 5:21, we're told to "Test everything; hold fast what is good." Growth and discernment are like a self-feeding cycle, a precious circle. Where there is spiritual growth, there will be spiritual discernment.

Yet discernment is not a sort of hypercriticism that incapacitates your ability to appreciate and turns you into an embittered watchdog only sniffing out others' mistakes. Instead it's a holy call to discern what is pleasing to God and what's not (Rom. 12:1–2). It gives you a redemptive freedom to relish what is true and beautiful and simultaneously reject what is ugly and false. Discernment equals growth.

So How Do We Get Discernment?

In Ephesians 4, Paul connects growth and discernment for the church in Ephesus. He explains that as Christians learn from godly teachers, we will "grow up" in Christ and become less and less like undiscerning children who are "tossed to and fro by the waves and carried about by every wind of doctrine, by human cunning, by craftiness in deceitful schemes" (v. 14). Instead, as we increase in maturity and wisdom, we will also increase in discernment. And as we do that, we "grow up in every way into him who is the head, into Christ" (v. 15). There's that beautiful, self-feeding circle again—growth motivates discernment which fuels growth which motivates discernment which fuels . . . you get the point. We see that in action in Ephesians 4.

So if discernment is needed to spiritually grow up, how do

we get it? Ultimately, like everything else good in our lives, God is the One who gives it to us (Dan. 2:21). His Spirit works in our hearts and effects lasting change. But he's also given us the responsibility of seeking and finding discernment. In Ephesians 5:10, he says, "Try to discern what is pleasing to the Lord." There are two big ways we do that.

Look and Learn in God's Word

God is the source of all that is right and true and worthy. He is the rock-solid foundation of discernment, so what better place is there to look for it than in his Word? At the beginning of Proverbs 2, it says that if you receive and study and love God's true words, he will give you discernment. When we set our minds on the things of God, we immerse ourselves in what is perfectly right and, in the process, protect ourselves from deception (Matt. 16:23).

God has written down his truth in Scripture, and we have unlimited access to it. By studying it, we're able to use it as an objective standard and measuring stick to evaluate the teaching we encounter. If you want more discernment, read the Bible. If you want to grow, read the Bible.

Ask God for Discernment

The second way to gain discernment seems both childishly simple and tiredly cliché—pray. But God is the one who gives us discernment, so we *should* ask for it. If we want to grow, we *must* ask for it. That's what Solomon did when he became king of Israel. God appeared to him in a dream and said, "Ask what I shall give you" (1 Kings 3:5). It was an unqualified invitation.

Solomon replied with great weight and humility,

> O LORD my God, you have made your servant king in place of David my father, although I am but a little child. I do not

> know how to go out or come in. And your servant is in the midst of your people whom you have chosen, a great people, too many to be numbered or counted for multitude. Give your servant therefore an understanding mind to govern your people, that I may discern between good and evil, for who is able to govern this your great people? (1 Kings 3:7–9)

He was a brand-new king. He could have asked for political power, victory in battle, popularity, fame, or unfailing success. Instead, he asked for the most valuable thing he knew of—discernment. Take a page out of Solomon's playbook and humbly and earnestly ask the Lord, the truth giver, to give you discernment. In James 1:5, we read, "If any of you lacks wisdom, let him ask God, who gives generously to all without reproach, and it will be given him."

God is the source of truth, so if you want to know what is right, go to him. Express your desire to obey him through discernment and ask that he would mature you in this area.

Discernment in Practice

If you are a Christian, the gospel means you *will* grow. And if you're growing, the gospel means you *will* exercise discernment. But exercising discernment in the real world can be tricky. While God's Word is infallible, man's teaching is not. And teaching doesn't just come from a pulpit. It comes from books, from screens, from schools, from music, from culture—basically, from everywhere. We meet it daily, and our God-given responsibility as Jesus-followers is to tell the difference between the kind that is true and the kind that's false.

I want to look a little closer at three human-directed media through which we grow (and must consequently exercise discernment in): books, music, and sermons.

Read to Grow

Like everything in our lives, the gospel deeply affects what we read. It redefines our evaluation of books, pressing upon us the need to be careful and watchful readers. At the same time, it frees us to grow through books as we appreciate God's grace manifested through his creatures. Blogger and author Tim Challies says, "Find me someone who has changed the world and who spent his time watching television and I'll find you a thousand who read books instead."[1]

Books are teachers, sometimes tough, sometimes gentle, sometimes comforting, sometimes convicting, sometimes disturbing, sometimes life changing, sometimes practical, sometimes profound. They expand our minds and horizons, banishing the temptation to tunnel vision. They teach us more about the world and more about the Bible and more about people and more about joy and more about holiness and more about eternity and more about relationships and more about sin and more about grief. They make us more intelligent and empathetic. They make us sharper reasoners and more critical thinkers. Books make us better.

C. H. Spurgeon said this very thing, "Give yourself unto reading. The man who never reads will never be read; he who never quotes will never be quoted. He who will not use the thoughts of other men's brains, proves that he has no brains of his own. You need to read."[2]

What should we read, though? A phrase that has helped me is this: "Read widely yet selectively." So I don't want to read books from only one genre or time period. That will skew my vision of God's broad and diverse truth and his grace and gifting in human lives. I want to read theology, biography, literature, history, memoir, ancient, modern, and so on. But I want to be a discriminate reader and read *selectively*. I want to discern what's the best, what's the most beneficial for my soul, and what is richest and most rewarding. Not all books are created equal. Discernment should compel us to both open and close book covers. Never be afraid of books. They are not masters, only tools.

Eleven Books I Love

Here are eleven books that have been powerful tools in my growth. (Perhaps you should consider looking back on the books that have most shaped your life and creating your own top list.)

Desiring God by John Piper

To Kill a Mockingbird by Harper Lee

The Holiness of God by R. C. Sproul

The Chronicles of Narnia series by C.S. Lewis

The Valley of Vision edited by Arthur Bennett

The Gospel by Ray Ortlund

The Godly Man's Picture by Thomas Watson

Amazing Grace by Eric Metaxas

Lizzie Bright and the Buckminster Boy by Gary D. Schmidt

The Freedom of Self-Forgetfulness by Timothy Keller

Holiness by J.C. Ryle

Listen to Grow

The fact that books are teachers is pretty obvious. The fact that music is also a teacher may not be. But it's true. Lyrics communicate ideas, and those repetitive ideas have pervasive psychological and spiritual effects on us. The gospel then must guide our listening.

It does this first by giving us parameters to enjoy music responsibly, not to restrict us but to protect us. Words and ideas in song can stifle our joy, upset our peace, crack our contentment, tempt us to lust, or make us slack about sin. At the same time, the right words can comfort us in suffering, stir up our affections for Christ, convict us of sin, and lift us up in encouragement. We should be engaged listeners, asking if songs edify us and mature us in Christ. That doesn't mean we're barred from listening to secular music (there is rich truth in some), but it should cause us to consistently ask ourselves if what we're listening to really and truly brings honor and praise to God (1 Cor. 10:31).

Bob Kauflin, a Christian pastor and musician from Kentucky, preached a sermon to students a few years ago on listening to music for God's glory. He offered six words and ideas "to help us think more concretely and biblically about the music we listen to." I think they're especially helpful for us.

- *Submission* (Prov. 19:20). As kids, our calling is to first obey our parents (more on that in chapter 8), and a big part of that is submitting ourselves under their authority. That encompasses submitting our entertainment. We can't listen to whatever we want without their approval. Our listening should be a gracious act of submission to their commands and teaching.
- *Content* (Phil. 4:8). Music overlaid with lyrics that exalt or glory in sin won't help us grow spiritually, no matter

how catchy the melody is. Think about the words you're putting in your mind.

- *Associations* (Prov. 22:3). If a song is associated with a particular person, place, or emotion for you, it can lead to temptation. Be aware of that.
- *Time* (Prov. 13:20). We spend a lot of time listening to music. Is that time aiding your gospel growth or stunting it?
- *Fruit* (Prov. 14:14). What fruit does the music you listen to produce in your life? Is it good or bad? Ask yourself if the music you listen to makes you frustrated, ungrateful, or irritable—or does it inspire you in godliness?
- *Conversion* (2 Cor. 13:5). It's important to remember that only Christians can exercise discernment in music (or any sphere of life). God is the One who gives us the ability to tell between truth and deception, so it's only through spiritual eyes that we can view (and enjoy) music rightly.[3]

The gospel also guides our listening by giving us the ability to genuinely appreciate music. My family loves music deeply, and we're an eclectic cocktail of different styles and artists. Between the four of us, we run the whole gamut—classical, country, pop, rock, rap and hip-hop, hymns, dance. These diverse styles represent how our individual personalities are emotionally affected in different ways by different music. And God created the medium of music to do that. Throughout all of Scripture we see people expressing and reflecting on their emotions through song (Exodus 15; Isaiah 12; Psalm 98). That's a gift.

Martin Luther loved music. Just read his words from a foreword to a collection of chorale motets: "I, Doctor Martin Luther, wish all lovers of the unshackled art of music grace and

HOW TO EVALUATE THE MUSIC YOU LISTEN TO

Am I submitting to my parents by listening to this?

Is the content true and edifying?

Do I associate this music with something pure or godly?

Is the time spent listening to this music aiding my growth?

What kind of fruit is being produced in my life by this music?

Am I viewing this music through a spiritual lens?

peace from God the Father and from our Lord Jesus Christ! I truly desire that all Christians would love and regard as worthy the lovely gift of music, which is a precious, worthy, and costly treasure given to mankind by God."[4] Luther knew the happy truth that the gospel gives Christians freedom to express and appreciate the grace of God through music. At the same time, it gives us a unique capacity to grow through it.

Pay Attention to Grow

Zack Zehnder was just an ordinary pastor in Mount Dora, Florida, until Friday, November 7, 2014. Wearing a green t-shirt with "50 Hours" written in a speech bubble, the then thirty-one-year-old pastor stepped behind his pulpit and delivered the longest sermon in history. He preached the entire Bible in 53 hours and 18 minutes.

What was the hardest part? He says:

> The preparation was by far the hardest part of the speech. . . . My goal was to preach through the entire Bible, from Genesis through Revelation. So, I picked out 50 different stories/topics and arranged them chronologically. From there I went through past sermons and tried to fill in the topics. I had notes and manuscripts for 35 out of the 50. So I had to fill in the other 15 just like any other sermon. All in all, this was about 2 years' worth of preaching for a normal pastor who preaches every week.[5]

Perhaps this will give you a little more grace for the length of your pastor's message this Sunday! While we don't hear fifty-three hours of preaching every weekend, as young church members we do still hear (shorter) sermons weekly. That's a part of gospel culture, faithful preachers regularly teaching, explaining, and applying God's Word to his people. Listening to those sermons is a profound way God has enabled all Christians to grow spiritually, including us teenagers. Eric McKiddie writes: "Teenagers in whom God is at work do not cringe at a gospel-centered sermon from the Bible. Rather, they receive it with power and joy, even if it causes them to suffer."[6]

If sermons are a catalyst for our growth, then we ought to devote serious consideration to how to listen better. Tony Reinke writes, "The life and health and growth of our souls are tied to how well we listen. We are wise to periodically evaluate our own hearing of God's word. If we listen with carelessness, we can drift away from God."[7] I think of careful sermon listening as a three step "P" process: (1) prepare, (2) pay attention, and (3) practice.

THREE STEPS TO LISTENING TO A SERMON

1 — Prepare. Plan for the sermon by resting well, spending time in Scripture before the service, and fighting the urge to zone out or daydream during the message.

2 — Pay attention. Practice discernment and ask yourself questions throughout the sermon, like "What is the main theme of the Scripture passage? What are the main truths the sermon communicates? What do I learn about God? What do I learn about sin?"

3 — Practice. Apply the message to your own life.

The first step (**preparation**) requires an extra "P"—planning. We prepare our bodies by getting a good sleep on Saturday night and making sure we're restfully alert Sunday morning; we prepare our minds by diligently fighting the urge to zone out or day dream; and we prepare our hearts by fixing our affections on Christ. An easy way to do this is to read his Word before church. I've noticed that when I do this (even if I only spend a little time), my heart is happier in Christ, kinder to others, and, yes, more receptive to the sermon.

The second step in sermon listening is to **pay attention.** This is where we see discernment play out—but as my mom likes to call it "discernment with a little 'd.'" If you are at a biblically grounded church, you shouldn't be listening to criticize or unfairly evaluate your pastor. You should come to his sermons with the preconception that you will learn and grow. Still, you should pay careful attention to what he's saying and ask discerning questions like, "What is the main theme of the Scripture passage? What are the main truths the sermon communicates? What do I learn about God? What do I learn about sin?"

This smoothly leads into the final step—**practice**. As you might expect, this is the stage where you apply the message. If you've been asking yourself questions about what God's Word says and what the main point of the sermon is, this shouldn't be too difficult. Ask now, is there a sin you need to stop? Is there a fruit of the Spirit you need to grow in? Have you been viewing God's character incorrectly or incompletely? Is there someone you need to forgive? Is there someone you need to ask forgiveness of? How does this change school tomorrow? A sermon shouldn't be a mere exercise in mental discipline. It should make a real difference in our everyday lives. It should help us grow.

Discernment will play an inevitably bigger role ("a capital 'D' role" as my mom would say) when you're listening to other verbal teaching, such as lectures, podcasts, or online sermons. Think about whether this teaching is an accurate interpretation of God's Word or a twisting of truth. Think about whether the teacher/preacher talks more about God and his wisdom or their own experience. Think about whether the teaching is motivated by doing more and being better or living a grace-centered, gospel-focused life. Think to grow.

Grow Up and Live

Growth doesn't happen by turning our minds on autopilot. It happens through consciously, intellectually, spiritually, eagerly engaging with the ideas we encounter. It comes from sifting through the good and bad that surround us and choosing what is true so we can do what is right. *Discernment changes everything.* As Jesus-followers, our entire lives are different because of what God says is true and what he says is false. For us, discernment and growth walk hand in hand.

As they do, we demonstrate that we're spiritually alive. We grow up and live or we don't. There's no in between—no wobbling, waffling, or wavering. The apostle Peter confirms our calling: "Grow in the grace and knowledge of our Lord and Savior Jesus Christ" (2 Pet. 3:18a). Keep learning about him, Peter says. Keep living for him. Keep reading about him. Keep singing about him. Keep hearing about him. Keep pursuing sanctification. Keep maturing.

Grow up, friends, and live.

• • •

Our Growth—Discussion Questions

1. What do you think C. H. Spurgeon meant when he said discernment was the difference between "right and almost-right"?

2. Why is a lack of spiritual discernment such a big deal in the world today? Why can't we just trust that everything labeled "Christian" is truly honoring to God?

3. As you think about your current music playlist and evaluate each song based on the "six words and ideas" (pages 104–5) are there any songs that need to be deleted? What about other forms of media—TV, movies, podcasts, video games? Is any song, show, movie, game, or podcast more important than obedience to Jesus?

7

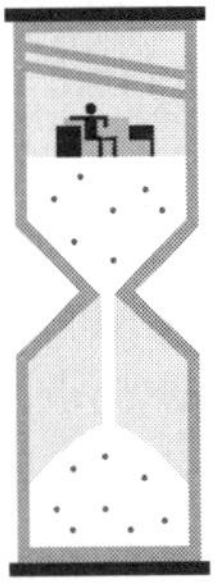

OUR TIME

It seemed like William and Jonathan couldn't have been more different if they tried. William was an only child, born and raised in affluent England. Jonathan was all-American, a pastor's kid from Connecticut with eight siblings. As a teenager William was a hard core partier who did his best to ignore God. Jonathan was a teenaged Jesus-follower who preferred nature and solitude to socializing. William couldn't care less about academics. Jonathan enrolled at Yale when he was thirteen. William wasted his teen years. Jonathan did not.

But William didn't waste the rest of his life. During his twenties, God saved him and impressed him with two important thoughts, thoughts that would bind him and Jonathan together. The first was that *life is short*, and the second was that *time is important.* William later lamented his lost teen years and resolved in his diary, "To endeavour from this moment to amend my plan for time. I hope to live more than heretofore to God's glory and my fellow-creatures' good."[1]

William's last name was Wilberforce, and he went on to spend the next forty years of his life serving Christ and working to abolish slavery in England. No one could say he wasted his life.

What about Jonathan? Jonathan too was obsessed with using time rightly. When he was nineteen he started writing down resolutions about how to live most to the glory of God. Resolution #5 read: Resolved, never to lose one moment of time; but improve it the most profitable way I possibly can. Resolution #7 was: Resolved, never to do anything, which I should be afraid to do, if it were the last hour of my life.

Jonathan's last name was Edwards. He went on to preach a sermon that started America's Great Awakening and become one of the most famous preachers and writers America has ever known. No one said he wasted his life either.

What's the Big Deal with Time?

Christians talk about time a lot. We're told to redeem the time, do hard things, and not waste our lives. Most of us have heard it a hundred times, and we're familiar with it to a fault. It's one of those concepts every Jesus-follower agrees on, but when it comes to daily practice, we are lost. We say and post and read the words but realistically live like we don't believe them.

We agree that the gospel changes who we are. It changes how we relate to the church, of course. It changes our disciplines, how we think about sin, discernment, reading, music, sermons, social media—check, check, check. But what to do this morning? That's where we get stuck. How does the gospel change my Saturday? That's where we've fallen into the trap of selfishness, and suddenly how we spend our time looks just like everybody else. We're drowning in busyness, wilting in laziness, or lodged in limbo. We need help.

But before that, let's back up a minute and ask: *Why do we even need to have this conversation?* Why is the topic of time such a big deal? First, because time is tremendously important. Jonathan Edwards argued that time is even more valuable than money. His reasoning was that money lost can be regained, but time lost never can. Those five minutes here and there add up into days and weeks and years. They add up to your whole life. How you spend today has an eternal impact.

Furthermore, God commands us to use our time well. Ephesians 5:16 calls us to make "the best use of the time because the days are evil." We live in an idolatrous age, and God's Word demands that our lives be different from those around us. It calls us to invest our minutes and hours in pursuits that bring honor to Jesus instead of temporary pleasure to ourselves (Col. 4:5).

Finally, and perhaps most important, our time is not our own. We are only stewards of this life, and we are accountable to God for what we do with it (1 Pet. 4:10). That is the profound truth we have lost. We've forgotten that our role in time usage is not master but manager. God is the One who has given us this life, and it is very much his. We don't have the liberty to spend our time however we'd like. Just as he's entrusted us with a measure of money and a degree of talents, we are only caretakers of his possessions. And we will answer for what we do with them.

How exactly do we spend his time?

How to Waste Your Time

Jonathan Edwards had an intense fear of wasting time. Like, scary intense. Reading his resolutions always sobers me. I mean,

HOW TO WASTE YOUR TIME

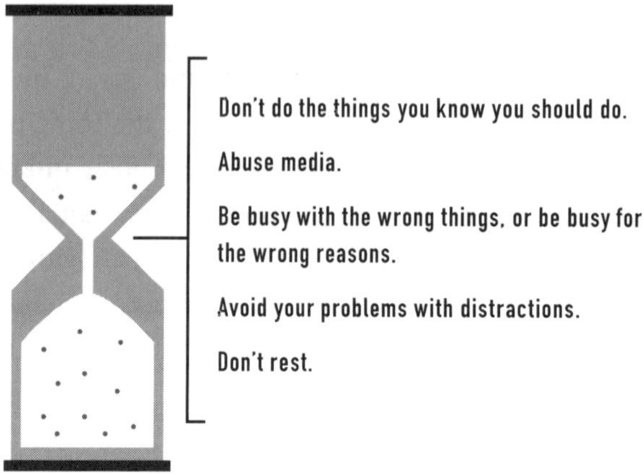

what nineteen-year-old writes, "Resolved, never to do anything, which I should be afraid to do, if I expected it would not be above an hour, before I should hear the last trump"? But Edwards got something we too often don't. He knew that life is short and only meaningful if it's lived for God's glory. He understood that wasting time is a direct result of taking our eyes off the gospel.

The problem is that we *do* take our eyes off the gospel, and that means we do waste time. Every day, in fact, we waste time. There are certain time traps we fall into again and again. Let me show you.

We Waste Time When We Don't Do the Things We Should Do

As Christians, we are called to a life of hard work and good deeds, and we are lazy when we neglect responsibility and loiter instead in mediocrity. Every day there are a thousand things we should do. From the mundane to the momentous, we have chores, homework, jobs, and opportunities to read, play with our siblings, treasure a sunset, wash the dishes, pray, write, exercise, pick up milk at the store, and pursue the fruit of the Spirit (Gal. 5:22–23).

In Ephesians 2:10, Paul writes, "For we are [God's] workmanship, created in Christ Jesus for good works, which God prepared beforehand, that we should walk in them." Paul underscores the truth that we are the very creations, the *images*, of an infinitely good God, and we were thus created to do good. And God has prepared in advance these good works for us to do. We waste time when we don't look for those good deeds—or when we find them and choose not to do them. James goes so far as to say that if you know what you should do and you don't do it, that's sin (James 4:17).

There are ordinary opportunities for kindness and service around us all the time. We just have to take action and do them. When we miss out on them, we can't get them back. Don't waste time by disobedient inaction. Seize the chance to do good for God's glory.

We Waste Time When We Abuse Media

Here it is—the obligatory media talk, where I list for you the statistics from the million dollar studies that show how the typical teenager watches 20 hours of television a week and how we'll have seen over 350,000 commercials by the time we turn eighteen.[2] That doesn't include the dozens of hours we spend online every week or the numberless minutes on our smartphones. And this doesn't even get into the nitty-gritty breakdown of social media—how much time on Facebook, Instagram, Twitter, Snapchat.

Don't get me wrong. These statistics can be helpful in certain contexts. But for us? Telling me that a faceless team of experts say I watch too much TV in a week is neither beneficial nor impactful. Chances are that I already know that. I know that I'm wasting time when I put off good works to mess around on Pinterest or watch a movie instead of doing my devotions.

But do I realize that seemingly innocuous time spent on those things can be actually sinful? Do I realize that when I abuse my minutes, I will have to answer to God for them? I could be changing the world right now, changing my life, but instead I'm sitting here wasting it. Do I really know that? I don't think so. It doesn't sink in that I'm accountable for all the time I waste on media. In the moment, all I'm thinking is that one thing leads to another, and time just, you know, gets away from me.

And full disclosure—I'm not using "I" to make you feel better. I specifically, personally have this problem. A few years ago my parents and I did an experiment where I recorded every minute I spent on the computer, keeping track of how much was for school and how much wasn't. After a few weeks we sat down together and looked at the results. The numbers left me shocked and ashamed, but also humbled and burdened with a desire to be more careful. They taught me that those few minutes here and there tally up fast. They tally into hours. And hours tally into days.

Try it sometime. Keep a notebook by your computer. Or download Toggl, a free time-tracking app. Get someone to hold you accountable. It won't be the most fun thing you do in your life, but you will find yourself different after it. Sometimes we all need reality checks.

We Waste Time When We're Busy with the Wrong Things or for the Wrong Reasons

In and of itself, busyness is not sinful. We can be busy with the right things for all the right reasons. But busyness *can* become sinful. Just ask William Wilberforce. Before he was saved, Wilberforce was crazy busy. After his conversion, though, Wilberforce looked back to see what his life really was—time busy on gluttony, gambling, sexual promiscuity, crude joking, getting drunk, and talking about a hundred things that just didn't matter. He referred to those years as "the most valuable years of life wasted, and opportunities lost which can never be recovered."[3] You may not be getting drunk at parties every weekend, but I'm guessing that sometimes you are busy with the wrong things.

I'm not talking about a job or school or even time spent with good friends or your family. I'm not talking about time spent cultivating godly habits. I'm talking about time spent going somewhere you shouldn't go, spending time with someone you shouldn't be spending time with, or pouring your time into pursuits that are either (1) sinful or (2) not worthwhile in light of eternity.

I'm too often guilty of falling into the latter category. You have to know that I am an obsessive person. When something new captures my interest I throw my whole being into it. I'm liable to let it consume me. A couple of years ago, this is what happened with murder mysteries. I discovered the British mystery novelist Agatha Christie at the same time I started watching an old murder mystery show on TV. The stories were riveting, the characters colorful and witty and arresting. I loved them. I was devouring murder mysteries by the dozen, gobbling them up in books and movies and on TV. I even had the genius idea to throw a murder mystery party, the pièce de résistance to my obsession!

Then one night everything changed. After reading an Agatha Christie novel before bed, I had a dream. At first brush, it wasn't too odd. All I did was make a drink—powdered chocolate milk or lemonade or fruit punch maybe. Naturally I woke up feeling thirsty and reached for the glass of water on my nightstand. As I lifted the glass to my lips, the smell hit me. I peered down to find thick, white goo swirling through the water, goo that had not been there when I went to sleep.

There was only one logical explanation—someone was obviously trying to poison me.

It was exactly like the movie I had just watched, the one where the woman poisoned that guy's glass of water and then he drank it in the middle of the night and died. And now it was happening to me! But why? And who? How did they pull it off? This was so exciting!

Then precisely one point five seconds later I saw the uncapped hand lotion bottle next to the water. So much for the poison and the mystery. See, I have a habit of sleep walking, and it seems that in my sleep I had squirted a bottle of lotion into the water (hence mixing the drink in my dream). It was a bit of a wake-up call (literally and figuratively) that I was spending too much time on murder mysteries. I had become so obsessed that I was even thinking death and poison in my sleep. So I took a break from the mystery novels and the show and the movies and began investing my time in other, better things. I still enjoy a good mystery now and then, but I no longer pour so much time into them.

What is your murder mystery? What are you doing today that is not worthwhile in light of eternity? Are you missing opportunities? Are you wasting good works? What can you change?

We Waste Time When We Avoid Our Problems

Sometimes we pursue busyness so that we can avoid an issue we don't want to deal with. We use busyness as an excuse to not have to reckon with reality. When we don't have time to sit down and eat dinner as a family, we don't have to deal with underlying resentment. When we don't have time to fill out college applications, we don't have to deal with our parents' expectations. When we don't have time to study with our friends, we don't have to deal with their emotional baggage. This kind of busyness gives us an appealing sense of escape.

But that is the absolute wrong way to handle our problems. Our lives are a part of something much bigger and more important than just us. Escaping our problems temporarily through busyness is only delaying the inevitable; we'll still have to deal with life. Problems don't get fixed by ignoring them. Putting them off ultimately does more harm than good—all it does is waste time and burden us with stress.

Of course, there are times when busyness is an entirely honest and valid excuse. But we have to check our hearts. Are we using busyness as a distraction, or do we genuinely have other responsibilities to take care of? What's at the root of our feelings and actions? Are we *really* too busy?

We Waste Time When We Don't Rest

There is a sharp distinction between laziness and rest. Laziness is selfish time spent in violation of God's command; it's self-absorption and idleness when we are called to work. Rest, on the other hand, is a God-given method of worship that allows us to refresh our hearts and minds. Laziness is bad, but rest is very, very good. Why do you think he gave us a Sabbath day?

There's some disagreement about what the Sabbath means for us today, but there's one thing almost everyone agrees on: God commands rest (Ex. 23:12). In the Old Testament that meant on one day out of seven the Israelites were not to do any work. In the New Testament, Jesus reinterpreted the command to reveal the heart of it—rest is good. God commands rest, esteems rest, and even modeled rest for us (Gen. 2:1–3).

Thus, when busyness keeps you from rest, you are violating God's command in your life. Rest is obedience. Jen Wilkin writes, "The God who grants us soul-repose commands our worship in the form of bodily rest. The worshiper is blessed in obedience."[4] When my family prays together at night, Travis frequently asks that the Lord would grant us good sleep so that we can wake up refreshed and ready to serve him anew in the morning. Travis understands what I often miss—rest makes us better workers and better worshipers.

How to Redeem the Time

If that's how to waste time, then how do we redeem it? Jonathan Edwards made a resolution "to live with all my might, while I do live." How do we do that? I want to share his same passionate desire to use all of life for God's glory. How does the gospel inform and shape our time usage? When we look at Scripture, we find God doesn't leave us in the dark. Rather, we find practical principles to seek his kingdom and redeem the time.

We Redeem the Time by Giving (and Doing and Being) Our Best

Dad often talks about how the Christian should be known as the best employee in his or her workplace. He doesn't mean they're automatically the most skilled or the most knowledgeable, but they are the hardest workers. They're the ones with the most integrity and the fiercest diligence. They're the ones who throw themselves heart-deep into doing the best they can,

because they don't do it just for a paycheck. They do it ultimately for the glory of God. This is directly in line with Paul's call: "Whatever you do, work heartily, as for the Lord and not for men" (Col. 3:23).

Sadly, our society has fostered a culture of complacency where teenagers are neither expected nor encouraged to work hard. It has become astonishingly easy for us to just get by, or to give a little less than our all and still get praised for it. Yet that's misusing time. We sometimes give less than our best, because . . . *why*? Because we're tired of doing hard work when no one else is? Because we feel like our efforts are wasted? Because others hate us for it? The excuses, though possibly true, fall short of gospel reality. In the end they evaporate, because the *A* on our paper is not the only thing God's looking at. He's looking at our heart. Diligence starts in the mind with an attitude that sets us apart from the world. God desires a heart that serves him with its very best.

We Redeem the Time by Enjoying God's Gifts

There are so many wonderful things in this world—art, autumn leaves, laughter, good conversations, root beer floats, flower gardens, summer barbecues, snowmen, sweatshirts, fairy tales, pie, playgrounds. God has given his children heaps of good gifts for our pure and utter enjoyment. Don't miss out on them. When you grow distracted from taking pleasure in what God has given you, you are misusing your time.

It's easy to get drawn into our own little bubble, where our own problems, worries, fears, and concerns surround us exclusively. It's easy to let them cordon us away from everybody else and the joys of real life. I struggle with this tendency to be self-contained, to bury my head too deep in textbooks or fret so much about my future that I just go through the motions and miss the magic of life. Don't do that. I have to intentionally choose to step out of the bubble, close the textbook, turn off my phone, shut down my computer, cut off the distractions, and embrace the wonder of life.

G. K. Chesterton poignantly assesses our condition: "We are perishing for want of wonder, not for want of wonders."[5] Just look around and breathe in life with your eyes wide open. Don't get so busy that you can't appreciate God's blessings. Joe Rigney, in his book *The Things of Earth*, adds to this: "Sometimes a pleasure is just a pleasure. Period. Full stop. God is honored by your enjoyment of it, your gratitude for it, and its fruitfulness in your life for the sake of the kingdom. So just receive the gift as one of the many pleasures at his right hand."[6]

We Redeem the Time by Sacrificing the Idol of Comfort

Most of us live a relatively comfortable life. In one sense, there's nothing wrong with that. God is the One who has placed you in your particular circumstance, and you should rejoice in what he's given you (see last point). But our comfort, like everything else we have (phones, houses, clothes, bodies), can become an idol. When we start elevating its status in our lives, we'll find ourselves building an altar to it.

And an altar is never unused. We'll begin to worship there and will begin to sacrifice to it. We might sacrifice sharing the gospel because it makes us feel awkward. We might sacrifice our church or godly friends or mentors. We might sacrifice giving or compassion. And we might embrace alternative things that smother us inside a bubble of comfort we refuse to burst.

Redeeming the time is choosing to burst that bubble. It's giving up the smoothness and easiness of comfort for the greater sake of the gospel. Because sometimes we need to give up comfort. Really. There are a whole lot of better things to do than just be comfortable—things like telling someone about Jesus, things like serving someone you don't like, things like fellowship, things like praying with someone, things like confronting a friend about sin, and things like standing up for what's right. Don't let comfort make you complacent.

We Redeem the Time by Living in Light of Eternity

In light of eternity, this life is just a drop in a ginormous bucket. Randy Alcorn says it like this: Picture eternity as a line that stretches to infinity, and this life as a tiny dot at the beginning of the line. The smart person, he points out, doesn't live for the dot. He lives for the line.[7] In other words, everything we do, how we spend today and tomorrow and every day until we die, should be lived with eternity in mind. It shouldn't be a mere afterthought but rather a kind of established truth that motivates our Monday mornings, a real truth for real life. It should fuel our desire to take hold of our lives with passion and purpose and to live for the kingdom of God on a daily basis. "Man is like a breath," David writes in Psalm 144:4, "his days are like a passing shadow."

Life Is Short, So How Will You Use It?

All this to say that our time on this earth is short. In his novel, *The Chosen*, Chaim Potok illustrated this through a father's wise words to his son, Reuven.

> Human beings do not live forever, Reuven. We live less than the time it takes to blink an eye, if we measure our lives against eternity. . . . I learned a long time ago, Reuven, that a blink of an eye in itself is nothing, but an eye that blinks, *that* is something. A span of life is nothing. But the man who lives that span, *he* is something.[8]

We each have a blink. We can waste it in sinful busyness or laziness or discontentment or distraction. Or the gospel of Jesus Christ can change how we spend our time. Living for him means we view our life as his. It means we seize life with intention and passion. It means we do, give, and be our best; enjoy God's gifts; sacrifice the idol of comfort; and live in light of eternity. It means we resolve with teenaged Jonathan Edwards to live with all our might, while we do live.

Time is of the essence. What will you do next?

• • •

Our Time—Discussion Questions

1. What specific areas of time wasting do you struggle with the most? What can you do to correct them?

2. Why does God want us to rest? Why is rest so important?

3. List some of the good, happy, ordinary gifts God has given you.

8

OUR RELATIONSHIPS

Throughout this book we've attacked this question: *What does it look like for teenagers to live a life transformed by the gospel?* We've seen how the gospel impacts our entire identity, our relationship with the local church, our sin and repentance, our disciplines, our entertainment habits, our learning and growth, and our time. I see only one place left to go from here: how the gospel changes our relationships with other people.

In some ways that's a hard thing to write about. My relationships and yours probably look pretty different. Personality, circumstance, and history all play their parts in shaping the particulars of our individual relationships and so make our perspectives unique. I don't want to project on you the specific aspects of my own relationships at the expense of alienating those of you who can't relate.

That being the case, what you'll find in the pages ahead is more principle and less practice. I want to do a sweeping Grand Canyon-sized view of Christ-centered relationships for us teenagers and then let you zoom in on what it means for your own life. I want to get the wheels in your brain turning, and let you apply these principles to your own relationships. This chapter then is whatever you make of it.

Relationships Are Really Good

But first, let me take you back to 1959 and introduce you to Mike Ferris. Mike has amnesia. He's opened his eyes to find himself at an empty diner, wearing an Air Force flight suit with no clue of who he is or why he's here. He leaves the diner, hoping to meet someone and at least figure out where he is. He walks along a dirt road until he reaches a small town called Oakwood. But mysteriously enough, this place is abandoned too. While there are signs of life everywhere—a bubbling coffee pot on the stove, lights on at the movie theater, water dripping in a sink—there are no people. Mike's worry grows, as does his confusion, as does his desperation. Where is everybody?

His fear slowly escalates into full-on hysteria, and he runs through the empty town in a frenzied panic, looking for somebody—anybody. But there's no one to be found. He finally collapses next to a crosswalk and pounds the WALK button, whimpering for help.

Yet things are not as they seem. In this episode of *The Twilight Zone*, Mike is not hitting a WALK button. He's hitting a PANIC button. And he's not in Oakwood. He's actually in a military facility, trapped in an isolation booth, where he's been for 484 hours and 36 minutes. Mike is an astronaut in training, being tested to see if he can endure the psychological stress of a trip to the moon alone. Oakwood and everything in it was a hallucination Mike projected because he simply could not endure the burden of loneliness. Without people, he literally went crazy. Emotionally, physically, mentally, and spiritually, Mike discovered that relationships are necessary—and not only necessary, but good.

We know this not because of the fictional Mike Ferris but because of the all-true God. It was this God who invented relationships (Gen. 2:18–22), and he invented them as a happy reflection of himself (Gen. 1:26–27). God is a relational being (think of the perfect and self-satisfied relationship between the three persons of the Trinity), and he made us to be relational beings too. Adam's need for Eve was not an unmanly weakness or fatal flaw. It was a simple expression of his humanity. People need people. That's the way God's world works.

Relationship is an unbreakable and unstoppable thread that weaves its way through the whole narrative of God's story. Inside each and every one of us there is a fundamental desire for community and a similarly basic fear of loneliness. In his mercy, God has given us people to satisfy that desire. He's given us families. He's given us friends. He's given us classmates and coworkers. He's given us churches.

Intuitively we know there's something wrong with isolation. Proverbs 18:1 confirms that intuition: "Whoever isolates himself seeks his own desire; he breaks out against all sound judgment." That's because God's kingdom is not built around loners; it thrives and grows on community. Think back to chapter 3—God reflects his glory through the community of the church. Relationships are rich blessings. Since the beginning of time, that's the way it was meant to be.

Relationships Are Crazy Messy

But like everything else in God's story, sin messed things up. It messed things up badly. When Adam and Eve disobeyed, the perfect relationships that were operating oh-so-smoothly in the garden of Eden suddenly cracked, sharply and deeply. First the relationship between man and God was broken. Then the relationship between man and woman was broken. Like the rush of ugly pouring out of Pandora's box, relationships swiftly became discolored with shame, conflict, jealousy, and bitterness. Sin made relationships messy.

Today we still have to deal with that messy invasion of sin. On this earth we will never have perfect and peaceful interaction with people. In light of that, there are certain dangers we face in our relationships, two in particular.

The first is *idolatry*. There's a lurking temptation in us to put people on pedestals, a desire to let them occupy places in our hearts meant only for God. The world screams this at us, urging us to put our trust in people. And let's be honest—it's a persuasive cry. People we love greatly are around us all the time. They're touchable, seeable, huggable. But the gospel reveals that they're ultimately empty idols, unable to give us soul-deep satisfaction. They're unable, because they're not God. Only he can deliver the all-satiating fulfillment we crave.

The second danger relationships pose is *selfishness*. This is idolatry too, but it's a specific kind—self-idolatry. This idolatry puts us on the throne in our relationships, giving us an excuse to treat people as vehicles for our happiness. It makes our relationships about personal rewards and single-focused gain. It makes us demanding instead of kind, jealous instead of grateful, arrogant instead of humble. It breeds such an obsessive self-focus that we irrationally arbitrate ourselves as the good and glory in our relationships. It takes without giving.

Relationships Have Only One Purpose

I think we all can see the worldly attraction of those relationships. They're easy. They're comfortable. They're all about us. Breaking free from that mind-set is a lot harder. Selflessness is a lot riskier. But when has following Jesus ever been about ease and comfort? Never. In fact, Jesus promises us the opposite is true (Mark 8:34). Rejecting idolatry and selfishness is more difficult, but it's a direct implication of the Spirit's work in our lives. With a gospel lens, we see them as temptations to fight instead of embrace. Where we once walked in selfish idolatry, today we resolve to walk a narrower path. This path is characterized by a new purpose, one that supplants selfishness and marks every relationship we have. And right here, folks, this is the main point of this chapter, the central take-away:

> The gospel transforms our relationships by giving us one purpose in them: *to become more like Christ.*

Just five words. The gospel means every single relationship you have should be about becoming more like Jesus as you do good to others. In Scripture, there is one clear way this plays out—love. No matter who you're interacting with, whether you're on Facebook or face-to-face, no matter what kind of relationship you have, the gospel calls you to love people (Rom. 13:8).

We're called to love sacrificially. "[Love] does not insist on its own way" (1 Cor. 13:5). Love gives up for the good of others, things as little as a piece of chocolate cake and as big as a life-changing dream. It unfastens its eyes from itself and sets out to serve with gratitude.

We're called to love with genuine joy. "[Love] is not irritable or resentful; it does not rejoice at wrongdoing, but rejoices with the truth" (1 Cor. 13:5–6). Love in our relationships looks like true happiness for others and celebration (not resentment) at someone else's triumphs and delights.

We're called to love patiently. "Love is patient" (1 Cor. 13:4). Love, Paul says, doesn't get frustrated when it's waiting on a sibling, angry when its plans are upset, or annoyed at busy baristas. It meets people where they are and bears with them.

We're called to love with encouragement. "Therefore encourage one another and build one another up, just as you are doing" (1 Thess. 5:11). Encouragement holds out open arms for others, to build them up. Love naturally reaps encouragement—texts sharing verses, phone calls to pray, coffee dates to talk about Scripture or life or troubles or joys, and sometimes just our silence, even just our presence.

A Glimpse of Relationships in Real Life

You are called to love like this in every relationship you have. Reject idolatry, reject selfishness, and love each person you meet with sacrifice, genuine joy, patience, and encouragement. That being said, different relationships can provide different challenges, opportunities, temptations, and responsibilities unique to their particular contexts. In my life there are four kinds of relationships that capture my time and call me to love in different ways. They're the relationships with my parents, my siblings, my friends, and the opposite gender. I'm guessing you have most of these, or at least very similar, relationships too. As we look at them together in the next few pages, I hope we'll be inspired to take real steps to pursue greater Christlikeness with the people we know.

Parents

Logan is a thirteen-year-old Jesus-follower, and he's trying to be faithful in all of life. But when it comes to his relationship

HOW TO ACT TOWARD YOUR PARENTS

- **Learn from their wisdom.**
- **Obey their authority.**
- **Mature from their discipline.**
- **Be grateful for their care.**
- **Treat them with genuine kindness.**

with his parents, that's especially difficult. They've never been close, and he consistently struggles to honor them. I understand how he feels—not in the distanced relationship (my parents and I don't have any trouble getting along) but in the honoring. Almost every Christian teenager has heard the fifth commandment (Ex. 20:12), but we all wrestle with the challenge of living it out. It's one of the few calls in Scripture explicitly to young people, so I want to know this: *How exactly do we honor our mothers and fathers?*

Honoring starts with knowing who our parents are. I don't mean what their names are or who culture—or even you—thinks they are. I mean who God says they are. And the Bible gives us a pretty full and compelling image of Christian parents. They are:

- **Teachers** (Prov. 1:8–9). Parents are your primary instructors, the people who will vastly shape your most foundational beliefs. They teach you about God and everything else—sexuality, cooking, education, friendship, beauty, politics, etiquette, language. That's how God designed it (Prov. 13:1).

- **Authorities** (Eph. 6:1). Not every parent out there has legitimate authority over you, but *your* parents do. Honoring them is tied to recognizing that their authority is God given and meant to be taken seriously.
- **Disciplinarians** (Prov. 13:24). Since they're your authorities, your parents also have the power to discipline you. While discipline is inherently painful (for both you and them), they are called to it for your ultimate well-being. Discipline is the cornerstone of growth.
- **Individuals** (Gen. 1:27). Parents are people too. As obvious as that fact is, I'm guilty of forgetting it. My parents have an identity beyond Mom and Dad. They have dreams, desires, fears, full personalities, and plans. They are individuals too.

These gospel realities should inform exactly how we relate to our parents. Let me explain. First, if our parents are teachers, we should *learn from* them. They have a fountain of experience deeper and wider than ours, so heed their counsel and listen to their advice. Communicate with them and express your questions, fears, and struggles. As their students, we ought to be comfortable talking to them about absolutely anything. Even if it's awkward. Even if we feel vulnerable. After all, they're our parents.

Next, if our parents are our authorities, we should *obey* them. Honor fuels obedience. So we don't go to that party. We don't argue with our sibling. We do our homework. We obey *in everything*, even the pesky and painful commands, the humdrum and tedious ones. Even more, we don't obey out of a sense of embittered duty, with heavy hearts and ingratitude. We obey out of happiness. Your parents aren't just looking for the action; they want the right attitude.

• • •

Unfortunately, I have to give a brief side note: I recognize that, because of sin, not every parent is a godly and compassionate authority, and not every parent wants his or her child to follow Jesus. For the teenagers who are struggling to obey in those kinds of situations, let me encourage you with this plain but painful truth: by submitting to your parents, you are submitting to God. Your earthly honoring reflects your greater heavenly One.

Obey your parents as much as you can, until you reach a point where you are asked to sin. Your obedience stops there but not before. And on the days when you wrestle with discouragement or frustration, remember you have a heavenly Father who is perfectly faithful, perfectly loving, perfectly kind, perfectly trustworthy, the perfect parent in every way. And he loves you with an unshakable love.

• • •

If our parents are our disciplinarians, we should *mature* from their discipline. Punishment is terribly uncomfortable, but if we learn its lessons, we are wiser people for it. Discipline shouldn't make us angry at our parents (though I'll be the first to admit, that's hard not to do). Instead, if our attitude is humility, it should make us *grateful* to our parents. Yet in my own experience, I've found that gratitude often comes later, when the sting of discipline has long dulled. What if we actually expressed gratitude a day later instead of a decade later? That would be a bold sign of maturity.

Finally, if our parents are individuals too, we should *treat them with genuine kindness*. They are as human as your friends and your coworkers. Pray for them. Laugh with them. Encourage them. Take them out for lunch. Write them a random note of kindness. Take out the garbage for them. Figure out their likes and dislikes and tastes and favorite things and foods and movies—and love them.

Siblings

Siblings are a strange phenomenon, aren't they? They're usually the people you love most in the world and at the same time the ones who annoy you most in the world. If you've been paying attention throughout this book, you've probably picked up that I have a brother named Travis. He's my only sibling, two years younger and, in many ways, very different than I am. But we're blessed to get along pretty well.

Sibling relationships vary vastly depending on age difference and personality. Still, whether your siblings are older or younger, saved or unsaved, close or distant, the gospel binds them together with you with one common thread. That thread is *looking out for their interests.*

In Philippians 2:3–4, Paul tells us, "Do nothing from selfish ambition or conceit, but in humility count others more significant than yourselves. Let each of you look not only to his own interests, but also to the interests of others." And then he uses the example of Jesus. Fellow teenager, if you want to be like Jesus, count your siblings as more significant than yourself.

So we say, "I'm going to put your needs and your wants and your happiness above my own." We say, "I'm going to give you the last brownie even though I really want it." I'm going to do your chore for you today. I'm going to help you with your homework. I'm going to babysit you with a cheerful heart. I'm going to change your diaper. I'm going to buy you coffee. I'm going to admit I was wrong and ask your forgiveness. I'm going to do life in a way that puts you above me and doesn't ask for anything in return. I'm giving up my interests and following Jesus's commands and example. Counting others as more significant than yourself is dying to your natural selfishness, a daily challenge to rely on the Spirit's strength to kill your sin.

Dying to ourselves also means we give up the longing to be right every time. We stop the argument with our brother. We're the first one to apologize to our sister. We don't always correct or criticize our younger sibling. Even if, in all those situations, we're the one who is right. The irony of life is that when we do everything we can to make people think we're smart, we usually end up looking pretty dumb. Think about the last time this urge led you into a fight with your sibling. I'm guessing it didn't end with them bowing gratefully to your superior knowledge and thanking you profusely for enlightening them.

Dying to the desire to be right is dying to pride. And that's something every sibling has to do every day.

Friends

When I was thirteen, I suddenly made a lot of friends. It happened when I joined a drama club. I immediately clicked with the core of kind and passionate teenagers, and we bonded over our love for theater and a shared desire to create meaningful conversations on the stage. We attended each others' birthday parties and threw cast parties and saw each other weekly at rehearsals. But three years later when I left the club, things changed, and the friendships began to fade. It's not like these friends just disappeared altogether, but the glue that held our relationships together (drama) melted. Without it, our "close" friendships fizzled out.

In contrast, there's Hannah. We've only met each other in person once, and she lives on the opposite side of the country, but I consider her one of my very best friends. Our grandparents went to church together and set us up to be email pen pals over seven years ago. Hannah is a fellow Jesus-follower and encourages me in Christ with every email she sends. I can go back to some of our earliest correspondences and read through all of her emails to find her prayers for me, her transparency, love for truth, and gracious accountability. Our friendship only gets stronger as time goes by.

The wisest man to ever live, King Solomon, thought friendship was a huge deal. He recognized that the people we spend our time with have a powerful, tangible influence over us. In Proverbs he devoted a heap of his counsel to the importance of choosing the right kind of friends and urged his son to spend time with people who were:

- just and kind (Prov. 1:10–19)
- pursuing righteousness (Prov. 12:26)
- wise (Prov. 13:20; 14:7)
- unconditionally loving (Prov. 17:17)
- close and committed (Prov. 18:24; 27:10)
- teachable (Prov. 9:9)
- level-headed and self-controlled (Prov. 22:24)
- honest (Prov. 25:18)
- trustworthy (Prov. 25:19)
- edifying (Prov. 27:17)

A tall order indeed, one no human being can perfectly fill. But there are friends out there who are pursuing all those good things. There were in ancient Israel, and there are today. Hannah is living proof of it.

Making godly friends is not always easy, though, especially when it comes to school. Kyra is sixteen and goes to public school. "At my school," she told me, "my sister and I are the only strong Christians there, so our other friends are non-Christians or they claim to be Christian but don't live that way." Luke is sixteen and goes to public school too. He admitted, "I would say that school as a Christian can be hard because of the temptations and how people only notice you for the bad things that you do. So that only makes it harder to say that you are a Christian." John is homeschooled but he agreed: "I probably have less friends than I would if I weren't a Christian."

I resonate with all of them. These days I don't have many friends either, yet Solomon seemed to think that was okay. We live in a culture addicted to convenience and speed, where there's so much pressure to be constantly going and doing and multitasking that we've sacrificed a handful of deep relationships for an ocean full of shallow ones. We don't have the capacity to be close to all two thousand of our Facebook friends. Solomon says, take the time to cultivate deep and godly friendships. Find the Hannahs out there who are going to build you up and bless you. Don't idolize the idea of popularity or status or convenience, but instead slow down and think about who you're spending time with.

You can't get past the first chapter of Proverbs before Solomon is giving his son advice about choosing friends. "My son, if sinners entice you, do not consent" (Prov. 1:10). Throughout the whole book he repeatedly warns his son to avoid "fools" (see Prov. 14:7, 16; 17:12; 23:9; 26:4–10; 29:9). These are the people who don't walk in wisdom. They say whatever they're thinking, think sin is a joke, mock obedience, tear others down, and pursue self-glory above all else. Do you know anyone like that? Solomon says, those are not the friends you want.

But that's not to say we won't (or shouldn't) be friends with non-Christians. It's impossible not to if you go to a public or private school or work at a secular business. You're around un-

THE KIND OF FRIEND TO LOOK FOR (AND BE)

- Just and kind (Prov. 1:10–19)
- Pursuing righteousness (Prov. 12:26)
- Wise (Prov. 13:20; 14:7)
- Unconditionally loving (Prov. 17:17)
- Close and committed (Prov. 18:24; 27:10)
- Teachable (Prov. 9:9)
- Level-headed and self-controlled (Prov. 22:24)
- Honest (Prov. 25:18)
- Trustworthy (Prov. 25:19)
- Edifying (Prov. 27:17)

believers every day. Yet Solomon reveals that our relationships with them can never be deeply and permanently close. Our life purpose, our future, our struggles and victories are so different from theirs, and we don't have a bond over the most important things that matter. Don't push these friends away or avoid them, but realize that, for the sake of the gospel, you can never share a heart-deep friendship.

My friend Isabelle is eighteen and once told me something very true: "While it's easy to have friends that you can spend time with, it is much harder to find those you can laugh with, cry with, pray with, and debate theology with. When you become a Christian, it's a bit like joining a special club. Certainly you still spend time and care for others outside of the circle, but you want to spend more time with those who are in the know."

Gospel friendships are a God-given blessing (Prov. 18:24). They make Christians wiser and stronger and more joyful Jesus-followers. They're hard to find, but they're an invaluable gift. Know that, and be grateful for them.

The Opposite Gender

Now we get to the fun part. Or do we? I think it's likely I'm about to disappoint you. I have no ten commandments for dating, no list of "appropriate" physical boundaries, no Hollywood-esque story about how the love of my life waltzed in and won my heart (at least, not yet). The thing is, I have no real specific tips and tricks to manage the inevitably awkward and fun relationships with the opposite gender.

Instead I have one word for you. It's a buzzword in Christian circles, and while some are always promoting it, others swat it away as stuffy and prudish. It has its lovers and haters. The word is *purity*. This little word has unquestionably changed how I interact with all the guys I know. This is why: *because of the gospel, the priority in my relationships with the opposite gender is to promote purity*. In other words, how I become more like Jesus in these relationships is to celebrate, protect, and display purity. It sounds simple and perhaps even obvious, but when you look at its relational implications, it gets a whole lot more complicated.

Promoting purity starts in your mind. It is born, bred, and exercised in your brain and begins with examining your thoughts, desires, and attitudes. When you're with a member of the opposite gender, what do you think about? Why do you think about it? When you're alone and daydreaming, who (or what) are you dreaming about? Do you actively, intentionally guard your thoughts from sexual immorality? These days it's popular to put pornography filters on our devices. But do we put these same filters (figuratively) on our minds? Are we diligent to avoid sexually-charged images, ideas, and entertainment?

The root of purity is a commitment to think about "whatever is true, whatever is honorable, whatever is just, whatever is pure, whatever is lovely, whatever is commendable, if there is any excellence [in it]" (Phil. 4:8). Only then can we act purely.

Once we change our thinking, we can pursue pure actions. Ask yourself the hard questions. When you're with a member of the opposite gender, why do you say what you do? Why do you dress how you do? Do you try to perform for the opposite gender's attention? How? Do you act based on culture's standard of purity or God's?

Purity is bigger and more pervasive than just yourself, though. We should be taking steps to not just protect our own purity but the purity of *the opposite gender*. It makes quite a difference when your focus shifts to someone else's heart instead of only your own. But that's a huge part of loving others—thinking about their interests, their thoughts, and their holiness. It makes you more conscious of dressing modestly (girls *and* guys), of avoiding inappropriately intimate settings, of setting boundaries on social media, of being held accountable, of fighting lust, of praying for your friends of the opposite gender. You can—no, you *must*—help others be pure.

Having friendships with the opposite gender is great. It really is. Boys and girls can learn a great deal from each other. But why does who-likes-whom always have to get involved? If your priority is to protect purity, then that should overshadow your every word, action, retweet, like, text, thought, and desire. Remember, all of our relationships ought to be contexts where we're becoming more Christlike as we do good to the people we know. Can you say that about your relationships with the opposite gender? Can I? If we can't, something has to change. And it has to change now.

Now It's Your Turn

At the end of the day, no relationship in our life is untouched by the gospel. Not a one. Every relationship should be about us loving like Jesus, serving like Jesus, encouraging like Jesus, and, like Jesus, glorifying God above all else.

And now we're at the end of this chapter. That means it's your turn. How will you apply these principles to your own life? Think about the next words you speak. Consider how you can be kind in the next hour. How can you serve someone? How can you encourage? Will you die to yourself—even when your sibling gets on your nerves tonight? Will you obey your parents? Will you build up your friends? Will you protect purity?

How will the gospel change your relationships today? Only you can answer that question.

• • •

Our Relationships—Discussion Questions

1. Which of the two dangers in relationships (idolatry or selfishness) do you struggle with more? How does being aware of these potential dangers help us fight against them?

2. What are some specific ways you can honor, encourage, and love your parents this week?

3. What do you think celebrating and promoting purity will look like in your life? Have you thought about dating, marriage, or even your own friendships with the opposite gender in light of the gospel?

EPILOGUE

Now that we're at the end, there can be no doubt: the gospel literally changes *everything*. From the tiniest pieces of life to the biggest, the gospel's reach extends over it all. And as this book comes to a close, let's be clear about one thing—when we're talking about the gospel, we're talking about God. *God* changes everything.

God is Creator, who gave us life.

God is Savior, who redeemed our souls.

God is refuge, who relieves our burdens.

God is Father, who forgives our sins.

God is King, who demands our service.

God is peace, who satisfies our longings.

God is wisdom, who guides our steps.

God is transformer, who totally, irreversibly, and utterly changes our lives.

There is only one response to a God like this: *worship*. Conclusions are all about asking, "What now?" Right here, this is the answer to your "What now?": Spend your youth (and every day of the rest of your life) in wide-eyed, soul-saturated worship. Fix your eyes on the life-giving, soul-redeeming, burden-relieving, sin-forgiving, service-demanding, all-satisfying, step-guiding, life-changing God. Be humble, be wonderstruck, be faithful, and throw yourself into a single-focused pursuit of this King of the universe. Take up your cross, deny yourself daily, and follow him.

God is at work in this generation. He's raising up young people to reject the status quo and risk everything to obey him. That's our generation. That's me. *That's you.* And this is our calling.

God changes everything. Now, teenager, go out and live like it.

ACKNOWLEDGMENTS

When I pursued writing this book, I had a naïve idea that it would be a fairly solitary process. Now I know that was a crazy idea. There were many people who played integral and powerful parts along the way. Thank you first off to Brett Harris, for publishing me on TheRebelution.com at sixteen, for nurturing my desire to write for fellow teenagers, for coaching me along the way, for working on my proposal, and for agenting for me. This book wouldn't be here without you.

Thank you to the entire team at Crossway for your willingness to publish me and your kindness and help throughout the whole process. Thank you to the designers, the marketing team, the copyeditors, and each person who so generously contributed to this project. You are full of integrity and deeply committed to Christ in a way I consistently admire.

Thank you to Dave DeWit for advocating for this project from the very beginning. Thank you for reading every chapter as I wrote it and giving me invaluable feedback. And thank you for being so open and transparent about the process for this publishing newbie.

Thank you to Laura Talcott for her kind and careful edits.

Thank you to all the friends who answered my many questions and gave such thoughtful, gracious, and engaged answers. Thank you to Hannah Scheltens for your friendship over the years and for the constant joy you've been in my life. Thank you to Grammy and Grampy and Grandpa and Grammy Dawn for modeling Christ and sharing in my happiness.

Thank you to my family at Gospel Light Baptist Church, for your texts and emails and prayers and cookies and encouragement all throughout writing this book. You are my family, and I'm constantly blessed by your love.

Thank you to Travis for providing me with so many illustrations for this book—and for building me that stand-up desk in the basement. I'm glad you were born, and I'm glad you're my brother, and I'm glad you teach me so much about following Jesus.

Thank you to Mom and Dad for everything—for reading every version of this book so many times, for your passion and persistent prayers, for your honesty and criticism, for your help with my terrible conclusions, for all the granola to keep me going, for giving me time and space, and for pointing me to Jesus at every turn. I mean it so much when I say, *you are the best.*

And since this book is first and last and foremost about the God of the universe, I am most grateful that he gave me this opportunity to write about him. It is for his glory I write, and for his glory this book exists. May it never cease to be so.

Soli Deo gloria.

NOTES

Chapter 1: Our Identity

1. Drew Dyck, "What Do Teenagers Need from Youth Ministry?" *Christianity Today*, June 21, 2011, http://www.christianitytoday.com/biblestudies/bible-answers/spirituallife/youthministry.html.
2. Jim Elliot, quoted in Elisabeth Elliot, *Through Gates of Splendor* (Wheaton, IL: Tyndale, 1981), 172.

Chapter 2: Our Story

1. Sinclair Ferguson, *The Whole Christ: Legalism, Antinomianism, and Gospel Assurance—Why the Marrow Controversy Still Matters* (Wheaton, IL: Crossway, 2016), 82.
2. Herman Bavinck, *Reformed Dogmatics: Prolegomena*, ed. John Bolt, trans. John Vriend (Grand Rapids, MI: Baker Academic, 2003), 1:138.
3. Jimmy Needham, "The Story (A Spoken Word)," by Jimmy Needham and Will Hunt, recorded 2014, on *Vice & Virtue*, NeedHim Music, http://jimmyneedham.com/music/.
4. You can see their work at www.iamsecond.com/films/.
5. John MacArthur, *Moments of Truth: Unleashing God's Word One Day at a Time* (Nashville, TN: Thomas Nelson, 2012), 352.

Chapter 3: Our Community

1. In this book I share memories of some of my family, friends, and acquaintances, and they have granted me permission to relate their roles in my memories to you. In some instances, where I was unable to ask permission, I've changed their names to protect their privacy. Jake, Peter, Alyssa, Bianca, and Logan are completely fictional, though they do represent teens in common situations today, including many I've met.
2. Kelly Bean, *How to Be a Christian without Going to Church: The Unofficial Guide to Alternative Forms of Christian Community* (Grand Rapids, MI: Baker, 2014), 36.
3. Stephen Nichols, *Welcome to the Story: Reading, Loving, and Living God's Word* (Wheaton, IL: Crossway, 2011), 65.
4. Cathy Lynn Grossman and Stephanie Steinberg, "'Forget Pizza Parties,' Teens Tell Churches," *USA Today*, August 11, 2010, http://usatoday30.usatoday.com/news/religion/2010-08-11-teenchurch11_ST_N.htm.
5. Martin Luther, quoted in David Mathis, "Kindle the Fire in Corporate Worship," *desiringGod.org*, May 19, 2014, http://www.desiringgod.org/articles/kindle-the-fire-in-corporate-worship.
6. Bethlehem Baptist Church Staff, "The Meaning of Church Membership and Accountability," *desiringGod.org*, February 1, 2001, http://www.desiringgod.org/articles/the-meaning-of-membership-and-church-accountability.
7. Melody Zimmerman, "One Thing Christians Often Miss When Picking a College," *The Rebelution* (blog), March 16, 2015, http://therebelution.com/blog/2015/03/one-thing-christians-often-miss-when-picking-a-college/.
8. Francis Schaeffer, *The Church at the End of the Twentieth Century* (Downers Grove, IL: InterVarsity, 1970), 107.

Chapter 4: Our Sin

1. John Owen, *The Mortification of Sin in Believers*, ed. Richard Rushing, abr. ed. (Edinburgh, UK: Banner of Truth, 2004), 5.

2. Wayne Grudem, *Christian Beliefs: Twenty Basics Every Christian Should Know*, ed. Elliot Grudem (Grand Rapids, MI: Zondervan, 2005), 97.
3. Ibid.
4. Arthur Bennett, ed., *The Valley of Vision* (Edinburgh, UK: Banner of Truth, 1975), 124.
5. Ibid., 150.
6. Ibid., 160.
7. Ibid., 134.
8. Jon Bloom, "Success Can Be Perilous," *desiringGod.org*, January 13, 2010, http://www.desiringgod.org/articles/success-can-be-perilous.
9. Jonathan Edwards, *Sermons of Jonathan Edwards* (Peabody, MA: Hendrickson, 2005), 120.

Chapter 5: Our Disciplines

1. Donald Whitney, "What Are Spiritual Disciplines?" *desiringGod.org*, December 31, 2015, http://www.desiringgod.org/interviews/what-are-spiritual-disciplines.
2. While other disciplines are implied or subtly commended in Scripture, these four are explicitly commanded. We are plainly and repeatedly told to immerse ourselves in Scripture (Josh. 1:8) because these are God's very words (2 Tim. 3:16) and to obey them we must know what they are (Matt. 19:14). We are also specifically commanded to know and memorize them (Deut. 6:6; Ps. 119:16), pray often (1 Thess. 5:17; 1 Tim. 2:1), and share the gospel (Matt. 28:19–20; Rom. 1:16).
3. Justin Taylor, "Reading the Whole Bible in 2016: An FAQ," *The Gospel Coalition* (blog), December 28, 2015, https://blogs.thegospelcoalition.org/justintaylor/2015/12/28/reading-the-whole-bible-in-2016-an-faq/.
4. David Mathis, "Warm Yourself at the Fires of Meditation," *desiringGod.org*, March 26, 2014, http://www.desiringgod.org/articles/warm-yourself-at-the-fires-of-meditation.

5. You can still read it for free at http://www.fbcdurham.org/resources /scripture-memory/ (accessed October 6, 2016), or you can purchase an e-book version on Amazon.
6. Thomas Manton, quoted in Mathis, "Warm Yourself at the Fires of Meditation."
7. Donald Whitney, *Spiritual Disciplines for the Christian Life* (Colorado Springs: NavPress, 1991), 94.

Chapter 6: Our Growth

1. Tim Challies, "10 Tips to Read More and Read Better," *challies .com* (blog), September 17, 2007, http://www.challies.com/articles /10-tips-to-read-more-and-read-better-0.
2. C. H. Spurgeon, quoted in Brett Harris, "27 Books Christian Teens Should Read (and Grownups Should Too)," *The Rebelution* (blog), February 24, 2016, http://therebelution.com/blog/2016 /02/27-books-christian-teens-should-read-and-grownups-should -too/.
3. Bob Kauflin, "Listening to Music for God's Glory," *worship matters.com*, November 13, 2008, worshipmatters.com/2008/11 /13/listening-to-music-for-gods-glory.
4. Martin Luther, quoted in Bob Kauflin, "Music—Gift or God?" *worshipmatters.com*, December 21, 2010, http://www.worship matters.com/2010/12/21/music-gift-or-god/.
5. Zack Zehnder, "This Guy Preached the World's Longest Sermon: The Whole Bible in 53 Hours," *The Gospel Coalition* (blog), January 8, 2015, https://blogs.thegospelcoalition.org/trevinwax/2015 /01/08/this-guy-preached-the-worlds-longest-sermon-the-whole -bible-in-53-hours/.
6. Eric McKiddie, "The Impact of Expounding God's Word: Expositional Teaching in Youth Ministry" in *Gospel-Centered Youth Ministry: A Practical Guide*, eds. Cameron Cole and Jon Nielson (Wheaton, IL: Crossway, 2016), 56.
7. Tony Reinke, preface to *Take Care How You Listen: Sermons by John Piper on Receiving the Word*, ed. Tony Reinke (Minneapolis: Desiring God, 2012), 2.

Chapter 7: Our Time

1. William Wilberforce, quoted in Eric Metaxas, *Amazing Grace: William Wilberforce and the Heroic Campaign to End Slavery* (New York: HarperCollins, 2007), 64.
2. "Media Literacy: Fast Facts," *Teen Health and the Media*, accessed June 29, 2016, http://depts.washington.edu/thmedia/view.cgi?section=medialiteracy&page=fastfacts.
3. William Wilberforce, quoted in Alex and Brett Harris, *Do Hard Things: A Teenage Rebellion against Low Expectations* (Colorado Springs: Multnomah, 2008), 54.
4. Jen Wilkin, "Of Summer's Lease and Sabbath-Song," *TheGospelCoalition.org*, June 16, 2013, https://www.thegospelcoalition.org/article/of-summers-lease-and-sabbath-song.
5. G. K. Chesterton, quoted in Bill Goodwin, "Wondering Why," *First Things*, December 13, 2012, https://www.firstthings.com/web-exclusives/2012/12/12/wondering-why.
6. Joe Rigney, *The Things of Earth: Treasuring God by Enjoying His Gifts* (Wheaton, IL: Crossway, 2015), 171.
7. Summarized from Randy Alcorn, *Heaven* (Carol Stream, IL: Tyndale, 2004), 420.
8. Chaim Potok, *The Chosen* (New York: Random House, 1967), 217.